D0217532

EDWARD SHORTER is a member of the Department of History at the University of Toronto, where he teaches modern European social history. Among his research interests are the history of protest among the French industrial working class and the transformation of lower-class sexual behavior in western Europe in the course of modernization. He is the author (with C.Tilley) of *Strikes in France, 1830-1968* and has contributed a number of articles to journals.

THE
HISTORIAN
AND
THE
COMPUTER

A PRACTICAL GUIDE

EDWARD SHORTER

University of Toronto

The Norton Library
W · W · NORTON & COMPANY · INC · NEW YORK

To Ann

Contents

v

Preface

This book is intended to guide historians in working with computers from the beginning of a quantitative study to the end. As an elementary manual, it is addressed to readers who have had no previous experience with electronic data processing, and who have only the vaguest notions of what quantitative history is all about. At the outset I emphasize that no preliminary knowledge of machine programming or of mathematics is required in order to conduct successfully this kind of research. And although some background in such disciplines as sociology, economics, or political science might prove useful, it certainly is not essential. This guide should permit the historian whose previous experience has been confined solely to Plain Old History to use modern electronic techniques.

Like most how-to-do-it manuals, this book starts with first things first. After two introductory chapters on quantitative history and on historians who have already worked with computers, we take up the design of "codebooks"—devices for getting the information in the historian's source onto punchcards. We then pass to the preparation and manipulation of these cards, going on to discuss the computer itself and how the problem of programming should be handled. This manual concludes with two chapters on analyzing the results of a quantitative project, proceeding from techniques for describing one's findings to intricate ways of identifying statistical relationships in the evidence.

Though scholars in other disciplines may find this work useful, it has been written with an audience of historians in mind. It speaks to their particular problems and concerns, to the kind of evidence historians most often work with, and to their reservations about employing the techniques of the social sciences. Moreover, the discussion is limited to data processing, which is only one of the applications historians may find for computers. Those researchers interested in the content analysis of texts will have to turn to other guides within the social sciences. Readers whose primary concern is with "information retrieval," such as the maintenance of bibliographical files, will also be disappointed in the present work. However, these are areas peripheral to the concerns of the great majority of historians.

Most of those who use this book will have been considering the evaluation of some quantitative source. Perhaps they are political historians, interested in the study of parliamentary voting patterns or of popular electoral behavior. Or they may be doing biographical research on a large number of individuals, such as the members of noble families. Many readers may have in mind projects in economic history, for example, the study of export and import patterns or the history of land transactions in some region. Still other readers will concern themselves with quantitative social history, studying the history of crime, of popular disturbances, of labor unions, or the development of population patterns as measured by census data. Other historians, to take a final example, will be working in demographic history, requiring some means of subjecting such lengthy numerical sources as parish registers to a detailed examination. This manual will tell scholars with these and similar interests how they may proceed in using a computer.

Some obligations must be acknowledged. Without the support of the Joint Center for Urban Studies of Harvard University and the Massachusetts Institute of Technology, and of the Canada Council, this book would never have been written. Among those who gave earlier drafts a critical reading are Cindy Aron, John Beattie, Glen Jones, Theodore Rabb, Peter Roosen-Runge, Judith Rowe, Ann

Shorter, and Stephan Thernstrom. Cecile Sydney typed the text and Joan Baker prepared the figures. Finally, I owe a special debt to Paul Robinson and Charles Tilly, who have contributed to this effort by suggesting changes in the manuscript and by giving me the benefit of their wisdom and their friendship.

EDWARD SHORTER

Illustrations

Introduction

This little book is intended to fill a gap in the literature on historical research. Nothing exists at present for the historian who wants to use a computer but has not the slightest idea how to proceed. The recent flowering of articles on quantitative history will be of little use to him, for excellent as they may be, they omit the specific discussions of punched cards and computer programs that he requires. Nor will the historian find the substantial literature on computer methodology and statistical analysis in other social sciences very convenient, for although a study of half a dozen books would ultimately qualify him for this new variety of research, as a total novice he would find much of this writing incomprehensible at first. He would also suffer the handicap of having to learn from examples suited to the problems and requirements of other disciplines.

It seemed to me that an audience existed for a book that would unite under a single cover all the historian need know in order to prepare information to be fed into an electronic computer, to make it do his bidding, and to analyze the figures the machine produces. It seemed to me further that the book should be written in as straightforward a manner as possible, eschewing the jargon that abounds in the social sciences, and elaborating in detail research methods and concepts with which social scientists become familiar as undergraduates or graduate students but to which historians, whose genteel humanistic training leaves them baffled by the flashing world of technology, are rarely exposed. Finally it seemed to me that in the course of my own experience with computer investigation I had accumulated by painful trial and error some practical lore that might be of use to other researchers about to begin quantitative studies.

The subject of computers and statistics for historians is of course right in the middle of the most recent of the new histories—quantitative history. Logically then, an appropriate starting place would be an appreciation of quantitative history, justifying its method of averaging and abstracting from large piles of uniform data in order to account for historical events. However, I shall forbear undertaking an elaborate defense of this genre, for two reasons. One is that there exists already a number of articulate rationalizations for the quantitative method, and to their arguments I have little to add.[1] Second, I intend this book as a practical guide, not a theoretical treatise, and a long intellectual justification of quantitative history would be pointless here, if only because readers who have fundamental biases against this mode of research are not likely to take the book in hand in the first place.

My purpose, then, is simply explanation and clarification, not justification. Among this volume's readers will perhaps be those scholars who, at a conference on urban history at the University of Leicester, listened to a discussion of card sorting techniques "with more awe than understanding," as the reporter tells us.[2] These are the readers to whom this book is addressed. My basic purpose is to whip away the veil of mystery that presently surrounds the computer in the eyes of most historians, so that even scholars who have fundamental reservations about the techniques and assumptions involved will at least understand how this sort of thing is done.

[1] See among others, William O. Aydelotte, "Quantification in History," *American Historical Review*, 71 (1966), 803–25; Stephan Thernstrom, "Quantitative Methods in History: Some Notes," in Seymour Martin Lipset and Richard Hofstadter, eds., *Sociology and History: Methods* (New York: Basic Books, 1968), pp. 59–78; and Charles Tilly, "Quantification in History, as Seen from France," forthcoming in a special issue of *Explorations in Entrepreneurial History*.

[2] H. J. Dyos, ed., *The Study of Urban History* (London: Edward Arnold Publishers Ltd., 1968), p. 147.

Yet a few remarks on the presuppositions of the quantitative method are necessary in order to understand the computer's requirements. Following this, by way of introduction, we will take up the question whether to use a computer at all in working with the data. Once all this is out of the way, we can begin with how one actually goes to work.

QUANTITATIVE HISTORY

Why quantitative history? What is wrong with the usual method of studying the past by isolating the origins and consequences of individual events? Those interested in quantitative history will find this procedure lacking in two ways. For one thing, the individual case the historian examines exhaustively may well be unrepresentative of the broader phenomena about which he wishes ultimately to generalize. Biographers, for example, are acutely conscious that the person they have selected for treatment might be perhaps not at all a "microcosm" of his social level, and that the forces that apparently shaped his life may just as easily have arisen from within the structure of his own personality as from the wider outside world. Collective biography is a form of quantitative history that promises to repair this defect in the biographer's material.

To illustrate this point in another way, urban historians have long been aware that the problems and conflicts of their particular town may be unique to that place, that all the world may in fact not be Philadelphia, to paraphrase the title of a recent paper on this subject. The dilemma of atypicality in urban history has threatened in the past to make that genre merely an elaborately titled cousin of "local history," about which professional historians are normally so scornful. Urban historians, in order to save themselves from suspicion of antiquarianism, have begun the quantitative study of cities, comparing one to another in order to separate the uniquely local from the widely typical.

Some social historians of the past, the discoverers of the now discredited category, the "rising middle class," could have saved themselves embarrassment by not embracing as characteristic of entire social groupings the few upwardly mobile families whose prominence caused a historical record of their activities to be preserved. Quantitative studies of social structure have demonstrated that European and American society abounded with families who moved downwards, and that the mobility of large numbers of lower-class people was blocked from the very beginning. In many other areas of historical research one sees how a decade or so of quantitative investigation has shed new light on traditional questions. Abstracting comparable features from a large number of historical events and comparing them one to another in order to determine what they have in common are modes of research used for many years in both America and Europe. They represent one basic dimension of quantitative history.

A second way in which quantitative history has challenged the "conventional" variety has drawn more notoriety. Rather than merely seeking new ways to answer old questions, many quantitative historians are recasting the questions as well. Specifically, they have been formulating historical problems in terms of the conceptual apparatus of neighboring social sciences. An old-fashioned quantitative historian might ask: How can I study the history of industrialization in Italy in order to say something new about Italian politics? The new-fashioned quantitative historian asks: How can the history of industrialization in Italy contribute to our knowledge of the process of industrialization in general?[3]

The point of this summary of fashions in quantitative history is that the computer may serve either group of quantifiers: the old-fangled variety who combine a passion for numbers with a taste for classical historical problems, or the new-fangled sort who see quantification as providing historical answers to basically unhistorical questions. These two approaches are clearly distinct, yet until now I fear the mention of the computer has caused them to be blurred together in the minds of many historians. Computer research has been

[3]Richard Tilly has recently made this point about German economic history, which in the twentieth century abandoned an interest in the laws of long-term economic growth for an obsession with the economic roots of political and cultural behavior; "*Soll und Haben*: Recent German Economic History and the Problem of Economic Development," *Journal of Economic History*, 29 (1969), 298–319. On the use of theory in American economic history see Thomas C. Cochran, "Economic History, Old and New," *American Historical Review*, 74 (1969), 1561–72.

so identified with sociology, political science, and economics that those historians who have been turning over in the back of their minds a quantitative project have been frightened away by the prospect of thereby becoming transformed into some misshapen hybrid.

The same with statistics. Either sort of quantitative project may profit from using statistical analysis, yet historians now tiptoeing about the edges of a quantitative source fall back in horror when mathematical treatment of the evidence is mentioned. The computer and statistics are neutral. They will not deviously compel the historian with a quantitative source to embark upon some path of explanation obnoxious to him.

The computer imposes upon both groups but a single conceptual requirement: the data must be put into a standard form. As we shall see in the chapter on codebook design, the researcher must devise ways to describe in a uniform manner a number of different historical events—in themselves enormously variegated and possessing threads of causation as intertwined as those in the Gordian knot. If the basic quantitative procedure is to accumulate the experience of many individuals, companies, towns, or crimes for the sake of comparison, the historian must make sure the "individuals" are comparable to begin with. Some readers will see in this requirement a basic philosophical stumbling block to quantitative history, arguing that no two events are really comparable, because each will have different origins and consequences. Other readers, however, will share with the social sciences the assumption that common elements of behavior unite all human actions, and press on to see how the computer may serve in the elucidation of this commonality.

WHEN TO USE THE COMPUTER

Given these considerations, should a historian with a quantitative project before him use a computer? Under what circumstances does the computer's economy in handling information and analyzing material outweigh the wearisome technical labor computer research involves? Many historians will have such small amounts of information that the trouble of using a computer simply will not be repaid. The analysis could better be conducted "by hand," as computer users

introduction   5 like to characterize unmechanized effort. In order to determine whether his own project would profit from computerization, the historian must have a rough idea what questions he wishes to ask of the data. If he wishes merely to measure magnitudes and dimensions ("parameters," as some say), he will need a large number of cases before computer analysis will be profitable. The interest of many historians in quantitative data will be limited to a few simple counts: how many charters were issued in one year, how many in another; how much crime was committed in Des Moines County, how much in Sioux; how many legislators came from rural backgrounds, how many from urban? Unless researchers whose quantitative questions are of this variety have huge amounts of information, they will have no need for a computer. One can much more easily resolve the questions by sitting down at one's card file, flipping through the cards, and counting with pencil and paper how many of this, how many of that. (Much later we shall discover that such tabulations are called frequency distributions; everybody produces them to begin the analysis.) After a few hours of flipping and sorting, the historian will quickly learn what he wants to know.

Herein lies the rub. In the course of doing quantitative research, many historians will discover that their questions are much more thoroughgoing than they had anticipated at the beginning of their project. Rather than wishing to know in aggregate figures how many of this, how much of that, they may discover they would like to see their data cross-classified. Rather than requiring the gross total of rural legislators, they would like to know how many such legislators came from large families, how many from small, how many enjoyed a formal education, how many did not. And they will wish to make these distinctions for urban legislators as well. In effect, they wish to have tables that break down their data simultaneously in two different ways. This tabulation of course is perfectly feasible with pen and paper. It merely takes more time and attention. Very quickly the scratch sheets begin to pile up, and new scales are added for new kinds of information, and new kinds of questions begin to form in the researcher's mind. Shortly the expenditure of energy threatens to mount into the monstrous when these trusted pen and paper methods are relied upon. At what point should the historian turn to the computer?

As a rule of thumb, historians who have fewer than two hundred cases, *and* who have for each case only a few pieces of information, will prefer to work by hand. Once, however, the number of items of data for each case increases to ten or so the historian will wish to think seriously about a computer. Each kind of information is called, in the trade, a variable. And if the number of variables increases arithmetically, the amount of labor in analyzing them increases geometrically, to paraphrase Parson Malthus. At issue really is not the absolute number of cases in the card box; it's how much is known about each. The number of tables the historian might potentially like to see is roughly half the square of the number of variables. Let us say the historian knows eight things about a legislator: his constituency, his party, the year he was first elected, the length of his tenure, his educational background, and his general orientation to business, labor, and social welfare. A systematic analysis might ultimately wish to compare each of these eight variables against each other. That is 28 tables, one comparing education with constituency, one comparing education with friendliness to labor, one comparing attitudes toward social welfare with amount of education. And so on. Now let us say the historian has information on some five hundred legislators. To produce each table, he will have to go through the file, inspect each card to see where the man in question falls, first in regard to one variable, then in regard to another; then he goes to the cross-ruled matrix on his desk and puts a little line in the appropriate box. He has to run through his file cards 28 times. Some of the boxes become smeared with little dots. The work sheets become dog-eared and tattered. Halfway through he discovers that some of his scales are wrong, and all the legislators are falling into one class, leaving the others barren. Isn't there a better way?

Here the benefits of the computer become manifest. With a few program instructions the machine will print out all these tables automatically. It will supply convenient summary statistics like averages and medians for the data. The output will be free of clerical error, an assertion few people who have labored into the night over voluminous hand-constructed tables and figures would confidently make. The pages that come from the computer's high-speed printer will be highly legible, free of confusing erasures and smears. And perhaps most useful of all, the user will be able to go back to the computer again and again if he discovers the first batch of output does not tell him quite what he wants to know, redesigning tables and re-arranging scales, selecting subpopulations from within his sample for special treatment and omitting others from some calculations. Pen and paper methods, on the other hand, often prove so wearying that the researcher seldom has the heart to go back and do the analysis all over again because of some minor deficiency.

The advantages the historian derives from the computer are all clerical, not intellectual. There is no question of letting the machine "do your thinking for you." The machine cannot think. Although I use such metaphors as "brain," "memory," and "the computer decides" from time to time as a way of designating intricate mechanical processes, let it be clearly understood that the computer is nothing more than a collection of switches that register "off" and "on." It has no independent intelligence of its own. The computer is not capable of a single intellectual operation beyond adding and subtracting numbers (it multiplies by adding and divides by subtracting), and shifting them from one register to another. When the reader realizes the computer is more like a giant clerk than a giant brain, to use Bert F. Green's analogy,[4] he will approach it with greater self-assurance.

Finally, by way of introduction, the basic steps involved in working with a computer should be mentioned. The core of this book, of course, is a detailed description of each of these main stages. Chapter 1, which discusses the research of other historians who have used computers, will ease us into this agenda.

BASIC STEPS IN COMPUTER USE

Having brought to hand the source material one wishes to quantify, the first step is to convert the data into a form the computer can read. This conversion is done with the aid of a codebook. A

[4]*Digital Computers in Research: An Introduction for Behavioral and Social Scientists* (New York: McGraw-Hill Book Company, 1963), p. 3; the Green book, moreover, is an excellent general introduction to computers and programming.

codebook permits the researcher to translate a wide variety of information—names, words, dates, amounts—into numbers comprehensible to the computer. The second chapter, "Designing the Codebook," tells how this is done.

Once the historian has his codebook, he proceeds to the second step, actual coding of his data. "Coding" means simply writing down on data sheets the numbers that the codebook dictates. The data sheet is a matrix of perhaps 30 rows and 80 columns. The symbols in each row will go onto a separate IBM card, each of the 80 columns corresponding to a column on the card. This stage is the subject of Chapter 3.

After he has filled out his data sheets, the researcher progresses to the third step of his project: keypunching the data and sorting the cards. The historian sits down at a keypunch machine and types onto IBM cards the information contained on the data sheets he has just filled out. The computer then reads these cards. Only through punchcards may the historian communicate with the computer, tell it about his legislators, his parishes, his unemployment statistics, or whatever, and ask it what he wishes to know about these matters. The keypunching finished, the historian will doubtless wish to fool around with his deck of data cards a bit before dispatching them into the maw of the machine. He will feed the deck into an accounting machine to have them printed out in a neat list; he will put them through a card sorter to arrange the deck in the desired sequence; he will be sure to copy his deck with a "reproducing punch" to have a second file for safekeeping. We shall discuss all of these steps in detail in the second half of Chapter 3.

Now the researcher is ready for step four, actually feeding his data deck into the machine and having it come up with substantive results. This operation is called programming. Computer programming is a skilled occupation, somewhat more difficult than taking shorthand, somewhat less difficult than repairing television sets. Most historians will, understandably, not want to occupy themselves with learning it. Nor is there any reason why they should. This is the one point in the project at which the researcher will have to enlist some outside help and hire a computer programmer for a brief spell. As we shall see, however, thanks to systems of "canned" programs, one of which is called DATA-TEXT, the historian can circumvent the trouble of hiring a programmer, and with no more than an hour or two of study write his own program. These matters will be examined more thoroughly in Chapter 4. Thus the programmer tells the computer exactly what operations to perform upon the historian's data, the machine whirrs, the little lights blink and flash, the printer attached to the computer crashes away, and in a jiffy the historian has his results. This brings us to the last phase of the process: interpreting the finished "output."

Two chapters are devoted to step five: analyzing the results. It is at this point that the technical, concrete business of punching cards and handing in jobs at the computer center gives way to more abstract, intellectual considerations of statistics. Many readers will find the very word "statistics" forbidding. Yet the techniques we shall discuss are readily comprehensible, indeed little more than a matter of common sense. I hope the reader will not be tempted to skip these pages, for the ultimate merit of computer research lies, it goes without saying, in how well the historian interprets what he learns, and Chapters 5 and 6 explain a few techniques that will make his job a little easier. The reiteration of a few caveats conclude this brief guide.

1

A Survey of Historians
Who Have
Worked with Computers

A review of some of the historical research already conducted with the aid of computers will give the reader a concrete idea of the possibilities the machine offers.[1] In the next few pages I will discuss briefly the work of several historians who have been experimenting with both card sorters and digital computers as analytic aids. A large body of historical research has also been undertaken by scholars from outside the profession, mainly political scientists, sociologists, and economists avid for historical data to provide a further dimension to their own nonhistorical concerns. I shall cite their investigations only occasionally, partly in order to keep the discussion a manageable size, partly to avoid augmenting the inferiority complex most historians acquire when confronted by these intruders.

POLITICAL HISTORY

In quantitative history, as within the entire discipline, the study of politics occupies a premier position. We should distinguish here

[1]One such overview is George G. S. Murphy, "Historical Investigation and Automatic Data Processing Equipment," *Computers and the Humanities*, 3 (1968), 1–13. The bibliographies in this journal attempt to keep track of published research done with computer assistance.

between analyses of legislative behavior, of electoral behavior, and of a large number of notables in general—an enterprise one might term "collective biography." Each of these three subgroups within political history is finding computer-oriented historians.

legislative behavior and the computer

The study of legislative behavior is a field ideally suited to electronic data processing. Because parliamentarians are prominent, biographical data on them are not hard to come by. Moreover, the two most often asked questions of the field dovetail neatly with the capacities of the computer for statistical manipulation: either how to find party alignments with "scalograms," or how to find correlations between the social and personal backgrounds of the deputies and their voting behavior. It is not surprising, then, that a number of researchers have started to analyze the parliamentary arena by machine.

In French history, Patrick and Trevor Higonnet have studied the legislature of 1846–1848 of the July Monarchy with the aid of a computer. They had information on some fifty different characteristics of around five hundred deputies, ranging from political allegiance, attitude toward the government and the Church, to the deputies' place of birth, social class, occupation, religion, income, and parliamentary experience. In addition, the Higonnets coded data on the characteristics of the legislators' constituencies, their population, the percentages of their rural dwellers, the wealth of the departments, and the number of industrial workers in the electoral district. Their information came from the standard parliamentary handbooks and other published compendia.

Machine analysis of these data led the Higonnets to several interesting conclusions. They found, for example, the much-touted corruption of the legislators of the July Monarchy to be negligible, insofar as such things may be judged from statistical observations. The religious beliefs of individual deputies, they discovered, were unimportant in determining political behavior. Simple totaling of deputies' occupations and social classes revealed the old-line French nobility to be more prominent in the politics of the Orleanist regime than hitherto imagined. Finally, the Higonnets were able to infer from their data several conclusions of fundamental importance to the political history of this period. They played down the inadequacies of political mechanisms in explaining the ultimate failure of Louis-Philippe's regime, emphasizing instead the gulf between the two segments of the political elite: the landed bourgeoisie and the traditional aristocracy. They also found the persistence of regional schisms important.[2] In coming to these conclusions, the Higonnets ventured into the realm of analytic statistics, using the chi-square—a statistic discussed below on pp. 115–19—to estimate the strength of associations between variables.

William O. Aydelotte has pioneered the use of computer techniques in the study of British legislative behavior. Aydelotte is trying to discover what basic philosophical divisions may have existed among the members of the House of Commons in the 1840s. To this end he has placed on IBM cards voting data for each of 114 roll calls between 1841 and 1847. Using a statistical technique called scalogram analysis, Aydelotte has checked for consistencies among the members' votes. On what kinds of divisions did a man vote liberal or conservative? May a hierarchy of such issues be constructed on which the political temperament of a member could be judged? Did merely one key division run through the House—political liberal versus political conservative—or were the members divided by several distinct philosophical principles? Preliminary results have led Aydelotte to conclude, for example, that the condition-of-the-people question was of relatively little concern to most M.P.s, and therefore not a guideline along which a liberal-conservative continuum may be built.[3]

[2]"Class, Corruption, and Politics in the French Chamber of Deputies, 1846–1848," *French Historical Studies*, 5 (1967), 204–24. A similar but much more ambitious undertaking is a study of politics under the Fourth Republic by Duncan MacRae, Jr., a political scientist. Analyzing 739 roll call votes taken from the *Année politique*, and 150 additional ones chosen at random, in addition to a host of other electoral and public opinion survey data, the author was able to make a number of important statements about political relations in Paris, and about the interrelationships between local problems and national politics. See *Parliament, Parties and Society in France, 1946–1958* (New York: St. Martin's Press, Inc., 1967).

[3]For a report of Aydelotte's technique and some first findings see "Voting Patterns in the British House of Commons in the 1840's," *Comparative Studies in Society and History*, 5 (1962–1963), 134–63.

A number of scholars are at work on machine analyses of legislative voting in the United States. For a long time students of American politics have seen the roll call votes of the Congress as a fertile source, yet until the advent of the computer the difficulty in analyzing them was forbidding. Recently, however, several such studies have appeared. Thomas Alexander, to take one example, studied the House of Representatives between 1836 and 1860 in an attempt to specify the way sectional loyalties eroded party bonds before the Civil War. For each of 13 congresses, Alexander fed into the computer information on how the congressmen voted on between 60 and 120 roll calls per session. Considering that perhaps 150 congressmen were present for each vote, the data file of the Alexander project assumed gigantic proportions. With the aid of scalogram analysis, the author was able to determine statistically the divisive power of sectionalism in the antebellum period.[4]

electoral behavior and the computer

For students of politics the other side of the coin to legislative history is how the electorate behaved. It is as important for historians to understand popular voting patterns as to describe political configurations in legislatures—but much more difficult. Whereas historians may apply their intuitive skills to legislative history, electoral history presents them with a depersonalized sea of numbers about as easy to comprehend intuitively as the pages of a telephone book. The key issues are the extent to which such matters as social class, ethnicity, and race are correlates of voting choice. The historians who now turn to these questions with the aid of computers will be able to give them definitive answers.

In German electoral history Karl O'Lessker has used a computer to challenge standard interpretations of the sources of Nazi victories

[4]*Sectional Stress and Party Strength: A Study of Roll-Call Voting Patterns in the United States House of Representatives, 1836–1860* (Nashville: Vanderbilt University Press, 1967); for a similar approach see Joel H. Silbey, *The Shrine of Party: Congressional Voting Behavior, 1841–1852* (Pittsburgh: University of Pittsburgh Press, 1967). Another machine-assisted study, this time of party cohesion before World War I, is Jerome M. Clubb and Howard W. Allen, "Party Loyalty in the Progressive Years: The Senate, 1909–1915," *Journal of Politics*, 29 (1967), 567–84.

at the polls in 1930 and 1932. O'Lessker analyzed the returns by district through a complex statistical routine, the multiple regression analysis. These calculations showed Hitler's supporters to be not the politicized middle classes identified by other scholars, but a combination of traditional rightists and former nonvoters. Only after the Nazis had become a great popular party did the German middle classes rush to vote for Hitler. The benefits conferred by the computer to this project lie not so much in the area of handling large data files—the actual data for such an analysis are modest in scope— but in performing elaborate statistical operations upon the electoral figures. Although pen and paper methods will quickly give the historian an overview of the gross returns, only the more elaborate procedures are likely to reveal hidden relationships in them.[5]

John L. Shover has recently applied computer electoral analysis to the political history of California. Although the Democratic party in that state experienced tremendous increases in voter registration in the 1930s, a shift could be noted several elections earlier. Shover asked which elections were critical in turning the corner for the California Democrats. To answer this, he computed correlations between each county's support of the Democratic and Republican parties in all Presidential elections between 1884 and 1940. High correlations emerge when the same counties continued to vote Republican (or Democratic) election after election, low correlations when the county vote began to drift from one party to another. By lining all these correlations up in a matrix Shover was able to distinguish either 1916 or 1924 as critical for the Democrats. Accordingly, he concluded that an "Al Smith revolution" did not take place in California during the 1928 election.[6]

Such research is only the edge of the wedge in electoral history. Data archives are now being established that will provide the source material for works on electoral behavior for years to come, and the information in these archives is accessible only by computer. Most important of these is the Inter-University Consortium for Political

[5]"Who Voted for Hitler? A New Look at the Class Basis of Naziism," *American Journal of Sociology*, 74 (1968–1969), 63–69.

[6]"Was 1928 a Critical Election in California?" *Pacific Northwest Quarterly*, 58 (1967), 196–204. For another example of research into American electoral history see Ronald P. Formisano, "Analyzing American Voting, 1830–1860: Methods," *Historical Methods Newsletter*, 2:2 (March, 1969), 1–11.

Research at the University of Michigan. The Consortium is the joint work of the Institute for Social Research of the University of Michigan and a number of other archives and educational institutions. Its purpose is to keep on file quantitative data of all kinds. The holdings of the Consortium have recently been expanded to include county-level data on all American elections for President, governor, and United States senator and representative since 1824. Thus a mind-boggling pile of information is now available on computer tapes for all such contests in every county in the United States over a period of 150 years. This amounts to some 20,000 individual elections involving over 100,000 candidates. The Consortium is further expanding its collection to include county-level information on various demographic, social, and economic characteristics since 1790. Further still, the Consortium will have on file all the roll call votes in the Congress from 1785 to the present. All this means that in the future historians who wish to work with such projects as the social determinants of the vote in a given election, or with legislative behavior projects such as the above-mentioned Alexander study, have but to write the Consortium, specify precisely what they need, and await its delivery in made-to-measure form on computer tapes. Historians in other national fields will regard their colleagues in American history with some envy.[7]

collective biography and the computer

One last area of "conventional" political history has seen an increasing number of quantitative studies carried out with the aid of modern data processing machinery: collective biography. This, as the name suggests, means approaching the sources with the perspective of a biographer, yet with the desire to escape the confines of the single case study, which biography has usually implied. Collective biographers study elites by collecting for a large number of people a limited but uniform amount of information, and then seeking out

[7]For information on the Consortium, as well as a programmatic look at American historians' uses of computers, see Jerome M. Clubb and Howard Allen, "Computers and Historical Studies," *Journal of American History*, 54 (1967), 599–607; Jerome M. Clubb, "The Inter-University Consortium for Political Research: Progress and Prospects," *Historical Methods Newsletter*, 2:3 (June, 1969), 1–5.

common features and patterns. A magisterial piece of research in this tradition is Sir Lewis Namier's study of English politics in the middle of the eighteenth century.[8] Namier investigated the members of Parliament without the aid of a computer; but other scholars have recently begun to use the computer for such studies.

One of the pioneering machine-assisted studies in the United States—Bernard and Lotte Bailyn's work on Massachusetts shipping early in the eighteenth century—may be classified as collective biography. The Bailyns wanted to make precise statements about Massachusetts shipping entrepreneurs of the period: how many ships on the average did each own? Did the typical shipowner tend to invest his capital in a small group of vessels, or did he join together with other investors in ownership? Did the urban Boston merchants monopolize ship transportation on the northeast coast, or did capital come from broadly based, geographically dispersed classes of investors? To suggest answers to these questions the Bailyns put onto punchcards the data in a Massachusetts shipping register for the 18-year period 1697–1714, ending up with a deck of some 4725 IBM cards, each of which represented a single investor's interest in a single ship. The subsequent analysis was then conducted with card sorting machinery, not with an electronic computer (although in judging the technical level of such an analysis, one must bear in mind that this was done in the late fifties, a time when the remainder of the historical profession thought a computer was somebody who kept score at baseball games). The Bailyns discovered that the ownership of Massachusetts shipping passed in these years from relative decentralization, involving many investors, each of whom had small shares in vessels, to concentration in a handful of risk-taking entrepreneurs centered in Boston. As time progressed, patterns of associations involving cooperation in shipping ventures also appeared. The Bailyns see these changes as evidence of "increasing economic maturity" in New England's commerce.[9]

Theodore K. Rabb has recently done a similar study of seven-

[8]*The Structure of Politics at the Accession of George III*, 2nd ed. (London: Macmillan & Co. Ltd., 1957).

[9]Bernard Bailyn and Lotte Bailyn, *Massachusetts Shipping, 1697–1714: A Statistical Study* (Cambridge, Mass.: Harvard University Press, 1959); see especially the authors' appendix on method, pp. 136–41.

teenth-century English shipping, using a digital computer rather than a mechanical card handling device. Rabb set out to analyze "one of the most striking transformations in economic history": England's great overseas commercial expansion around 1600. He wished to determine exactly who invested in the commercial companies of this expansion, whether they were primarily from the commercial classes or from the landed gentry as well, whether wealthy investors or small-scale capitalists. To this end Rabb plumbed the files of over thirty commercial companies, keeping a separate record of each investor. Having finally accumulated for some 8700 investors information about commercial involvement and social class, he was able to identify patterns of investment. In addition to prominent London merchants, an enormously heterogeneous group participated in commercial financing. Most important of these were the myriad small investors who hitherto have stayed in obscurity, brought to light only by the computer's singular capacity for ordering and recalling facts.[10] Other researchers have suspected this to be the case, but Rabb has been able to buttress hypotheses with important statistical evidence, calling his own effort at collective biography a kind of "namierization."[11]

One final piece of collective biography readers may find thought-provoking is R. Burr Litchfield's study of Florentine patrician families from the sixteenth to the nineteenth centuries. Interested in the rate of demographic survival of these aristocratic families, the author attempted by quantitative means to determine how many died out over the centuries and for what reasons failures to perpetuate the lineage took place. Litchfield recorded data on vital events in the lives of 2427 individuals born between 1500 and 1799, who together represented 21 old Florentine families. Genealogical registers and manuscript materials yielded data on birth and death dates, age at

[10]*Enterprise and Empire: Merchant and Gentry Investment in the Expansion of England, 1575-1630* (Cambridge, Mass.: Harvard University Press, 1967); Rabb's account of the course of his own researches, of his trials and tribulations in dealing with the computer, appears in a technical appendix, pp. 133–87.

[11]An Historical Data Center is being established at Princeton University, under the direction of Professor Rabb, for the purpose of assisting scholars interested in collective biography. The Center will provide expert technical direction and assistance in setting up such projects, designing codebooks, and in general making the novice conversant with machine-assisted research.

marriage, and family size. Litchfield discovered that the number of old families gradually decreased over the years. With fewer and fewer sons marrying, the number of collateral lines shrank until the existences of the families themselves were threatened. During the eighteenth century in particular the decline in vitality was marked, owing to rising ages at marriage and smaller family sizes. Litchfield ascribed this attrition to the failure of the municipal economy to grow over the centuries, a phenomenon that prompted the aristocracy to practice family limitation in order to preserve their wealth and status.[12]

"SOCIOLOGICAL HISTORY"

Whereas one group of historians has started to use quantitative sources and computers for the familiar history of politics and elites, another group of historians—their ranks heavily infiltrated by sociologists and political scientists—has begun using similar methods on "history from the bottom up." I am distinguishing here between standard history and "sociological history," the investigation of mass behavior and of popular classes. The most common areas of research within this field are the study of revolutions and mass movements, the study of social structure with special emphasis upon the city, and the study of demographic phenomena. The computer is being extensively used in all three kinds of subject matter.

the study of revolutions and mass movements

I would like first to describe some of the work being done currently on protest and revolutions in French history, aware of a certain parochial bias on my part in emphasizing France, for my own research interest is within this area. And I have followed other projects now in progress with much more attentiveness than I have devoted to, say, American electoral history. Nonetheless, reporting these projects

[12]"Demographic Characteristics of Florentine Patrician Families, Sixteenth to Nineteenth Centuries," *Journal of Economic History*, 29 (1969), 191–205. Professor David Herlihy is presently conducting a major study, using computer techniques, of the Florentine *catasto* of 1427–1428.

is justified if only because they may serve as models for other national fields in which the quantification has been less fast and furious.

Gilbert Shapiro, one of a growing number of researchers teetering on the borderline between sociology and history, is presently concluding a major work on the *cahiers de doléances* of the French Revolution. Unlike the other projects thus far mentioned, devoted to the study of quantitative numerical data, Shapiro is using the computer to study the textual content of documents. He employs what he calls a "concrete analytic code" to transfer the multifarious grievances mentioned in the *cahiers* into the memory of the computer. Thus, for example, the grievance: "We want to abolish all taxes, especially *la gabelle*" is placed on IBM cards with one set of unique symbols, the grievance "Increase access to the royal courts" with another. Shapiro has designed systematic ways of coding every imaginable grievance to be found in the *cahiers*. These data will permit him to make statements about the importance of one kind of grievance as opposed to another within the various revolutionary groupings, to answer the question: Was the revolution a single event, or were there many revolutions? For generations historians have puzzled over such problems associated with the Revolution as Tocqueville's paradox that the European revolution broke out first in France precisely because of the weakness of France's feudal system. This research provides a new quantitative dimension to their solution.[13]

Another sociologist-historian, Charles Tilly, is studying the revolutions and popular disturbances of nineteenth- and twentieth-century France. By searching the daily newspapers, archives, and secondary sources, Tilly has compiled a file of all important disturbances and riots in France between 1830 and 1860, and 1930 and 1960, with information on a sampling of disturbances in the years 1861 to 1929 as well. He has divided these violent incidents into two subgroups. For the larger group, numbering about 1200 dis-

[13]Professor Gilbert Shapiro of the Departments of History and Sociology of the University of Pittsburgh kindly supplied me with some of the internal documents his team has been using in this investigation. Of particular interest are a 100-page mimeographed booklet, "Quantitative Studies of the French Revolution: Concrete Analytic Code for the *Cahiers de Doléances*" (September 1, 1966), and a supplementary document by John Markoff explaining the use of the content codes.

turbances, Tilly has coded 25 pieces of information: location, date, number of participants, lives lost and damage done, and objectives and composition of the crowd, to mention some of the variables. For a smaller group, 550 disturbances in number, Tilly has gone much more deeply into the sequence of events, the precipitating circumstances, the formations involved, the presumed motives of the rioters, collecting altogether perhaps a hundred kinds of information about each incident. All these data have been coded onto IBM cards. With this material Tilly has been testing some hypotheses about the relationship between mass movements and politics. He believes that political action is the key to understanding collective violence, and suggests that people take part in disturbances in order to maintain established political rights or attain new ones. Tilly is testing these general hypotheses about collective action by studying the history of disturbances in France in particular. It goes without saying that finding the relationships within this enormous amount of material is possible only through computer processing.[14]

I am myself, in collaboration with Tilly, investigating strikes in France between 1830 and 1960. The essential source data are found in a publication of the French Labor Office, the *Statistique des grèves*, which lists every strike to have taken place in France (or at least to have come to official knowledge) between 1890 and 1935. The source gives information not only on the date, location, magnitude, and industry of the strike, but on the stated grievance of the workers, the number of establishments involved, the number of workers employed in these plants, the outcome of the strike, and how the dispute was settled. There are some 36,000 of these strikes. In addition, we possess sketchier information on disputes between 1830 and 1889, and aggregate statistics on strike activity since 1936. With these data we are trying to determine how the protest activities of the French workers developed and changed in the course of the industrialization of France. Preliminary findings indicate, for example, that strikes became increasingly politicized: They grew from

[14]For a preliminary summary of Tilly's findings see "Collective Violence in European Perspective," in Hugh Davis Graham and Ted Robert Gurr, eds., *Violence in America: Historical and Comparative Perspectives, A Report Submitted to the National Commission on the Causes and Prevention of Violence* (New York: Bantam Books, 1969), pp. 4–45.

occasional, lengthy, small-scale affairs waged as tests of economic strength to frequent, massive, brief symbolic demonstrations of working-class political power.[15]

A computer is useful in this strike study in two ways. For one thing, it permits us to manage this gigantic quantity of information —15 pieces of information on each of 40,000 strikes. The computer's prodigious skills allow us easily to classify these strikes by area, by industry, by municipality. They enable us to chart some essential dimensions of industrial conflict, like the average length, the normal size, and the typical level of worker participation. The computer facilitates comparisons of these dimensions from one industry or department to another. In short, it helps us to comprehend this unordered, hitherto unclassified mountain of information. Second, the computer makes possible an analysis of changes in patterns of strike activity by permitting us to see how external forces bearing upon the labor force shaped the actions of the workers. We are able to feed into the computer information on the distribution of France's work force for each industry in each department; we may collect quantitative data on the structure of industrial establishments, how many plants of what size are found in each industry within each department; information on union membership, on the level of urbanization, on electoral history—all this for each department at a number of points in time. The machine ingests this multitude of facts and—guided by the computer programs we supply—computes statistical associations between these various kinds of influences and strikes.

the study of social structure

The history of social structure is a second general area of sociological history in which scholars have been using computers. Current research emphasizes especially *urban* social structure, the city having been selected partly because the sources often define themselves in terms of single cities, partly because these researchers hold the city to be of particular theoretical significance. An enormous amount of research into this subject is currently underway, and I have space to mention only a handful of projects.

[15]These results are reported in "The Shape of Strikes in France, 1830–1960," in *Comparative Studies in Society and History* (forthcoming Jan., 1971).

A group of historians under H. J. Dyos are studying the Victorian history of the London suburb of Camberwell. They are trying to find out how the various social classes distributed themselves by neighborhoods, what the family structure of the community was, whether the middle classes were truly pushed out by the incoming working classes, and how these movements and distributions of population affected the politics of the area. To this end Dyos has collected information on a sample group of around 6000 households, and 27,000 individuals, spread out over the six censuses between 1851 and 1901. For each of these individuals or households, the researchers have collected information on age, birthplace, occupation, relationship to the head of the household, and marital status. The utility of these data, taken from census returns, is readily apparent.[16]

Merle Curti has led the way in computer-assisted research into the social structure of American communities. Indeed his work on Wisconsin's Trempealeau County was, alongside the Bailyns' monograph on Massachusetts shipping, the first machine-based project done in the United States. Curti's intellectual starting point was the ambition to put Frederick Jackson Turner's "frontier thesis" to a microcosmic empirical test. Did the American frontier stimulate the growth of democracy by providing the economic equality that laid the foundation for political equality? In order to answer this question, Curti put on IBM cards information about the age, occupation, birthplace, family size, literacy, and wealth of all gainfully employed people and householders in the county at several intervals between

[16]Dyos and A. B. M. Baker have recently reported on their progress; see "The Possibilities of Computerising Census Data," in H. J. Dyos, ed., *The Study of Urban History* (London: Edward Arnold Publishers Ltd., 1968), pp. 87–112; this paper is useful in that it demonstrates the typical problems encountered in applying machine methods to manuscript census data, and indicates some ingenious solutions to them. See also W. A. Armstrong, "Social Structure from the Early Census Returns," in E. A. Wrigley, ed., *An Introduction to English Historical Demography from the Sixteenth to the Nineteenth Century* (New York: Basic Books, Inc., Publishers, 1966), pp. 209–37. Lynn H. Lees has recently completed a study of the Irish in London in mid-nineteenth century, using a computer to analyze census returns. Some results from this are given in "Patterns of Lower-Class Life: Irish Slum Communities in Nineteenth-Century London," in Stephan Thernstrom and Richard Sennett, eds., *Nineteenth-Century Cities: Essays in the New Urban History* (New Haven: Yale University Press, 1969), pp. 359–85. Professor Lees graciously sent me a copy of her codebook, which is reproduced in the Appendix.

1850 and 1880—nearly 10,000 cases in total. In many instances he was able to follow the fortunes of individuals over a period of time. From his data Curti concluded that a great increase in the personal wealth of the citizens of the community as a whole, and especially of those who started with very little, had taken place. The rich became poorer and the poor richer. A host of such results led Curti to think the Turner theses about the links between economic opportunity on the frontier and political democracy did indeed explain developments in Trempealeau County.[17]

Whereas Curti investigated a rural community, numerous historians have been applying his methods and questions to urban ones. Notable among this research is Stephan Thernstrom's work on Boston from 1880 to the present. Using census returns, marriage license records, and birth certificates as his quantitative sources, Thernstrom has compiled a record of 8000 families that he follows over an extended period of time. These data will serve to help answer some of the classic questions of urban history: what differences existed in the social mobility of various ethnic and religious groups? Did the social structure of the city as a whole become more tightly knit as the nineteenth century gave way to the twentieth? How are the various measures of social mobility—occupation, residence, and income, to name three—interrelated with one another? And finally, to what extent is Boston typical of other American cities?[18]

One last study of urban social structure I shall mention is Sam Bass Warner's work on the history of Philadelphia. Using computers to analyze such sources as city directories and census returns for the years 1770–1780, 1830–1860 and 1920–1930, Warner was able to plot shifts in the distribution of occupation, income, and ethnic groups in the city. The high degree of occupational and ethnic segre-

[17] *The Making of an American Community: A Case Study of Democracy in a Frontier County* (Stanford: Stanford University Press, 1959); other scholars will find Curti's appendix on methods useful, pp. 449–58. I have reproduced his codebook in the Appendix.

[18] Thernstrom explains this project in "Quantitative Methods in History: Some Notes," in Seymour Martin Lipset and Richard Hofstadter, eds., *Sociology and History: Methods* (New York: Basic Books, 1968), especially pp. 73–74. For a further report see "Immigrants and WASPs: Ethnic Differences in Occupational Mobility in Boston, 1890–1940," in Thernstrom and Sennett, eds., *Nineteenth-Century Cities,* pp. 125–64. This volume contains other excellent illustrations of urban history conducted with the assistance of the computer.

gation he discovered led to the conclusion that an enduring tradition of "privatism" is one of the forces most responsible for the ruin of the American city.[19]

the study of demographic phenomena

The third line of inquiry emanating from sociological history is the study of population: demographic history. Few varieties of history lend themselves so easily to machine-assisted analysis, for demographic sources are invariably highly standardized and easily quantifiable—indeed already in numerical form. The registers of birth, baptism, marriage, and death may be transferred onto IBM cards, either in their entirety or on a sample basis, to serve a wide range of purposes. One such purpose is family reconstitution, which means following the demographic histories of a sizable number of families in a given community over the years. The computer reconstitutes the history of generations of families by collating mentions of the family name in the village's demographic registers.

In France a group of demographers guided by Louis Henry have brought family reconstitution a long way.[20] Among the first results of their labors is a study of the families of the Norman parish of Crulai in the seventeenth and eighteenth centuries. Available to the researchers was a rich fund of data, such as in the case of marriage registers, the place and date of the ceremony, the place and date of the publication of the banns, the ages of the newlyweds, the place and date of their birth, the occupation of the groom, the occupations and residences of the parents, and further biographical information about the in-laws. Data of this sort for some 6700 births, 1200 marriages and 3700 deaths were coded onto IBM cards, and from these the demographic history of the parish was reconstructed.[21]

Similar research is now in progress elsewhere in France. Marcel

[19]*The Private City: Philadelphia in Three Periods of Its Growth* (Philadelphia: University of Pennsylvania Press, 1968). Following an increasingly common custom, Warner has placed his computerized source data on file with the Inter-University Consortium for Political Research in Ann Arbor.

[20]The reference manual of these studies is Henry, *Manuel de démographie historique* (Geneva and Paris: Librairie Droz, 1967).

[21]Étienne Gautier and Louis Henry, *La population de Crulai, paroisse normande: Étude historique* (Paris: Presses Universitaires de France, 1958).

Couturier has been studying marriage certificates for the town of Châteaudun in the seventeenth and eighteenth centuries. J.-C. Perrot has been working on the birth, marriage, and death registers of the parish of Saint-Gilles in the eighteenth century. Several French research institutes have been collaborating on the family history of several Breton parishes in the nineteenth and twentieth centuries. French scholarship in these matters is at present easily the most advanced in the world.[22]

English demographic historians too have been pursuing family reconstitution in an effort to find the crucial social and economic determinants of birth and death rates, to establish the influence of different kinds of local economies upon vital rates, and in general to follow the course of the Demographic Revolution. E. A. Wrigley has recently reported some preliminary results of his family reconstitution studies in the town of Colyton in the period 1538–1837. Coding data in Colyton's baptismal and burial registers onto family reconstitution forms (FRFs), and then onto paper computer tapes, Wrigley has been able to calculate death rates for each age group, finding important differences in the rates among the three centuries. Family reconstitution studies are being conducted for a number of other English parishes as well.[23]

Here we end our review of existing research using computers. The projects I have cited are merely the tip of the iceberg. An enormous number of quantitative studies aided by electronic data processing equipment are now being carried out in North American institutions. Indeed, casual observations have convinced me there is not a major department on the continent in which fewer than two historians are

[22]These projects, as well as the nature of computer facilities available to French scholars, are discussed in Marcel Couturier, "Démographie historique et mécanographie électronique," in *Annales de démographie historique, 1966*, ed. Société de Démographie Historique (Paris: Sirey, 1967), pp. 57–68; and in several papers brought together under the title "Nouveau débat sur démographie historique et mécanographie électronique," *Annales de démographie historique, 1967*, pp. 29–55. See also Couturier, *Recherches sur les structures sociales de Châteaudun, 1525–1789* (Paris: S.E.V.P.E.N., 1969). Couturier describes his techniques and makes some important suggestions for employing computers in future demographic research on pp. 15–46.

[23]"Mortality in Pre-Industrial England: The Example of Colyton, Devon, Over Three Centuries," in *Daedalus: Historical Population Studies* (Spring, 1968), pp. 546–80.

now doing computer-assisted research. Some of these projects have stopped at the stage of card sorting and card counting machinery. Others have gone on to make sophisticated use of electronic computers and elaborate camputer programs. The point of this survey has been to give the reader an idea of what is now being done with computers, what kinds of projects are possible. The following chapters will enable the reader to design and execute his own project, departing if he so wishes from the paths other historians have already cut.

2

Designing
the
Codebook

The central problem in drawing up a codebook is to find ways of reducing people and events to numbers without distorting beyond recovery the distinctive colors and shades of their historical existences. Some tension, to be sure, is inevitable between the historian's instinctive preservation of the complexity of the individual case and the quantitative method's ruthless insistence that unique, discrete events be standardized. This chapter will point out ways of minimizing this tension. First, we will discuss the general principles and techniques of a codebook, what it is and how it works. Second, some specific techniques are presented for avoiding mayhem to the historical record. In the Appendix some codebooks of other scholars who have wrestled with this problem are reproduced, containing coding schemes the reader may find useful in designing his own research.

CODEBOOK PRINCIPLES AND TECHNIQUES

The codebook is designed to put information onto IBM punchcards, and so the first thing to do is describe the cards. The IBM card is the basic piece of technical equipment we encounter at this point. The reader will already be familiar with this device, having received his gas and electric power bills on them along with admonitions not to fold, spindle, or mutilate. As Figure 2–1 shows, the card is 80 columns across and 12 rows high. The top edge of the card is called the "twelve-edge," the bottom the "nine-edge," a first taste of the aerospace jargon one simply has to accept in dealing with these things. The computer reads the historian's data by checking electronically to see which positions are perforated in each column. Numerical data are entered in rows zero to nine of the card, a little square punched out of the card in the given column to indicate the particular digits. This is called the digit punching area. The top three rows of the card, called the zone punching area, give added flexibility, for a punch in one of these together with a punch in the digit area can represent letters of the alphabet and punctuation marks, as Figure 2–1 further demonstrates. (The 0 position is both a digit and a zone punch.) Thus 63 different symbols, numerical, alphabetical, and special, are available for each column of the card. Most historians, however, will prefer to limit themselves to the 10 standard numerals rather than get involved in multiple punching, for reasons I shall later make clear. Holes in the IBM card are punched according to the dictates of the codebook, to which we now turn.

The codebook is a document that translates evidence from the real world—of either a numerical or verbal nature—into digits, the

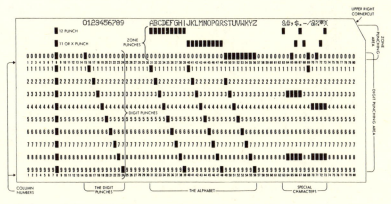

Figure 2–1 The IBM punchcard.

only data the computer understands. The following illustration, Figure 2–2, shows how the codebook works. On the left half of the

Figure 2–2 **Fields in the codebook.**

[Field]	Column	Code
	1	
	2	
	3	
	4	
	5	
A one-column field	6	Political affiliation
		1 = Republican
		2 = Democrat
		3 = Dixiecrat
		4 = Other
A three-column field	7–9	Year of birth (Enter last three digits of actual year)
	10	
	11	
	●	
	●	
	●	

page of the codebook appears a list of the columns on an IBM card. On the right half of the page appears a statement of what each of the numerical entries in these columns means. The machine reads only the numbers that are punched on the IBM card. The codebook tells the historian *which* numbers he should enter on the card so as to get information about historical reality into the computer's brain.

We can make things clearer with an example. Let us say the historian is studying a number of legislators. He possesses several pieces of information about each representative—name, constituency, date of birth, occupation, and political affiliation. The codebook permits him to give the machine all this information in a form it can understand. The deputies' politics, for instance. How do we code political allegiance? The historian first thinks out how many possible political categories and combinations there were during the period in question. To each of these he assigns a number: using the United States Congress as an example, a 1 would denote a Republican, a 2 a

Democrat, a 3 a Dixiecrat, and so on. As the machine processes each congressman's card, it will read a number for that man's political party. The codebook tells both the historian (so that he won't forget) and the computer that a certain number in a certain column on the IBM card means a datum of historical experience. A 2 punched in column 6 of a representative's card means that he is a Democrat. The computer knows it must always go to column 6 for information about politics. The historian knows what the codes in column 6 mean singly, because he has devised them. Thus does the codebook bridge the real world of history, at least as it exists in the mind of the historian, and the play world of numbers in the mind of the machine.

The blocs in which the data are grouped on the IBM cards are called *fields*. Political affiliation, to continue with the example above of the congressman, would occupy only one column on the card, a single digit alone being required for coding. Thus political affiliation is a one-column field. Other kinds of data on the congressman, however, would take up several columns. These columns together constitute a field, as Figure 2–2 illustrates. In order to code the year of the representative's birth, four digit positions (four columns) are necessary. (Actually, only three columns are necessary, because coding the first digit in the year is superfluous.) In order to code the congressman's name, we allocate a maximum of 15 digit positions. (With one letter per column, the arbitrary number of 15 lets us code quite long names.) To his state we assign a field of two columns so that each of the 50 states will have a separate number. To code Pennsylvania, for example, thirty-sixth on a list of the states, we put a 3 into the first column of the field (column 15) and a 6 into the second (column 16). The programmer will tell the computer that columns 15–16 are where constituency information is stored, columns 7–9 for year of birth data, and so on. Each different kind of information the historian wishes to give to the machine thus has its own separate field.

Figure 2–3 gives an overview of what we have just discussed. It shows how information from the source is first transferred to data sheets, with the aid of the codebook, and thence to IBM cards.[1]

---

[1] I have borrowed this illustrative device from Kenneth Janda's excellent handbook, *Data Processing: Applications to Political Research* (Evanston, Ill.:

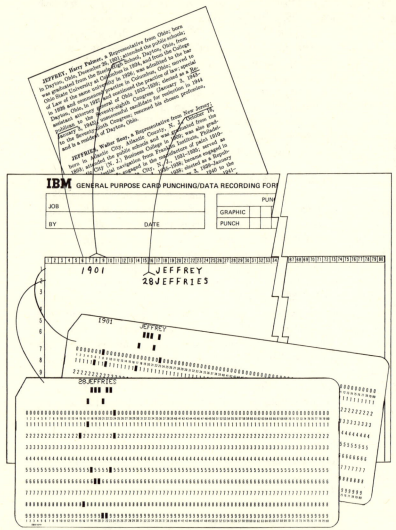

Figure 2–3 Transferring data from the source to IBM cards.

32

Data sheets are paper ruled to 80 columns across, as an IBM card has 80 positions, and perhaps 25 rows down. The actual codes to be punched on the IBM cards are first written in the little boxes of the data sheets. (Each congressman has his own row on the data sheet.) Then each row becomes a separate IBM card—thus there is a different punchcard for each man. The principle is overwhelming in its simplicity. Yet I have seen the eyes of numerous humanists glaze over when called upon to understand this first elementary step in data processing: "That's too difficult for me." Not really.

Most historians will want to incorporate several standard categories in their codebooks. To start with, in order to keep track of the individuals under study, the researcher should assign a unique number to each. Somebody working on the biographies of nearly a thousand congressmen would give each man a serial number, and his codebook allocate three columns to this field. The codes in these columns would run from 001 to 999. In the jargon of computer researchers the individual cases under investigation are called *units*. The unit of analysis may be anything—medieval charters, ships leaving Hong Kong harbor, members of Parliament—just as long as each unit has a unique number.

Another useful field the historian may wish to put in his codebook is the source of the data for each unit. This will not be a problem, of course, if all his cases are taken from the same source. However, if the researcher is pulling his data file together from a number of different sources, he will doubtless wish to preserve the provenance of each unit. In the case of the congressman, column 5 would become the source field. A 1 would be coded if the source were the *Biographical Dictionary of the American Congress*, a 2 if it were the *National Cyclopedia*, and so forth.

Many historians will be able to stop designing the codebook here. The historian is studying a large number of cases, but has so little information on each case that 80 columns are sufficient to record it. He has provided space on the IBM card for the consecutive number

Northwestern University Press, 1965), p. 27. Janda's book is the only practical guide to computer processing currently available for social scientists; it is particularly good on processing political data and on card handling machinery. The present book differs from Janda's in being written with an audience of historians in mind—tailored accordingly to their problems and requirements—and in encompassing a lengthy discussion of elementary statistical principles.

designing the codebook

of the unit, for source codes, and for whatever substantive information he possesses about each case. But in the example we have thus far been dealing with, the study of the thousand congressmen, 80 columns do not suffice. The historian has many pieces of information about each man, and cannot squeeze it all onto a single 80-column IBM card. What is to be done?

The wrong solution is to try to cram as much information as possible onto a card through multiple punching. Multiple punching means punching two holes in the same column in order to get a letter of the alphabet or punctuation symbol. It should be avoided, even though the historian, needing more codes than the digits zero to nine provide, will have to add additional columns onto fields. As Janda explains (p. 133), many pre-written computer programs reject multiply punched data; multiple punching also weakens the physical structure of cards, increasing the incidence of jamming; finally, more computer time is required for multiply punched data than for other data because editing and manipulating routines are slower. Similarly, the use of 11 and 12 should be shunned because the computer may interpret them as indicating that the data are algebraically positive or negative. (It may read a punch in the 12 row as a plus sign, a punch in the 11 row as a minus sign; the 11 punch is also sometimes called the X punch.) Nor should blank spaces be used as valid codes. These warnings do not mean that alphabetic data must not appear on the card, just that they must not be included with numerical data in the same fields. There are better solutions for data that exceed the capacity of a single IBM card.

The best approach is to spread the data for each unit out onto several punchcards. After the historian has exhausted the 80 columns on the first card, he may design his codebook to add additional fields to a second and a third card, indeed to as many cards as he wants for each case. He has only to construct his codebook so that the machine won't be confused as it grapples with this onslaught of multiple cards for each unit. Each card must have its own card number, and on each card should also appear the unique number of the congressman or the parish or whatever is under study. The card number should always appear in the same column on each successive card.

It may happen that each of the units in a multicard data deck will have different numbers of· cards. In some cases information will

designing the codebook

be missing, or the fields in a given card will not be relevant to the case at hand; or for some other reason the units will be of varying length. In such situations the historian may simplify the programmer's job by including in his codebook the field: "number of cards in this record." (*Record* is another word for *unit*). Let me suggest in addition that historians who have no more than a single card for each unit leave one column empty for an eventual future card number. It is always possible that the researcher will at some later date wish to expand his file of information.

We may illustrate how the card principle works with one of the sample codebooks reproduced in the Appendix, that for the Paris June Days of 1848. That codebook is designed to record information in dossiers on those arrested after the uprising—each person brought to trial being a separate unit (having a separate dossier). The data are distributed among four cards: one for basic biographical details, such as residence and arrival in Paris; one for data about family status; one for occupational information; and a final one detailing the disposition of the man's case in court. Thus for each unit there are four cards, card 1 for biography, card 2 for family status, card 3 for employment history, and card 4 for trial and sentencing. In the first column of each card one of those four numbers will be punched, and in the next five columns of each will be punched the number of the dossier, which is to say the unique number. The computer in fact needs to know only the number of the card, but the historian will need to have the dossier number affixed to each card for his own convenience.

When data for the sample codebook on the June Days are read into the computer, they will appear like this:

UNIT ONE	CARD ONE	FIELDS 1–37
UNIT ONE	CARD TWO	FIELDS 38–65
UNIT ONE	CARD THREE	FIELDS 66–102
UNIT ONE	CARD FOUR	FIELDS 103–115
UNIT TWO	CARD ONE	FIELDS 1–37
UNIT TWO	CARD TWO	FIELDS 38–65
UNIT TWO	CARD THREE	FIELDS 66–102
UNIT TWO	CARD FOUR	FIELDS 103–115

designing the codebook

To summarize the technical information presented thus far, there are cards and cards. "Card" is a generic name for the IBM card or punchcard; it also has the precise meaning of a bloc of fields grouped together on a punchcard. The data file consists of an accumulation of cards, and for each person ("unit") in the file there may be one "card" or several. Other terms we have encountered are equally elementary. *Code* means the numerical entries made on an IBM card. The *codebook* is the guide to which codes go in which columns of the punchcard. The *unit* is the individual case with which the historian is working, whether an individual, a city, an electoral district, or a share in a merchant ship. Each kind of information on which the scholar has data is called a *variable*, and is coded into a *field*, or bloc of columns on the IBM card. Now that the reader has acquired the terminology computer researchers use, he will not humiliate himself when he has lunch with them and discusses his project.

AVOIDING CODEBOOK PROBLEMS

As R. G. Collingwood has observed, historians expect to reach certain conclusions at the very beginning of their research projects. At the end they are often surprised to see emerge a set of explanations quite different from those originally envisaged. This element of uncertainty at the outset of a study is in the nature of things, for not until the researcher has all the evidence assembled can he pick out the wheat from the chaff. It raises, however, certain problems for computer research. The very essence of quantitative history is aggregation: lumping disparate cases together in the same category because of features they have in common. Yet at the beginning of a project how is the researcher to know which general categories will be useful and which not? Quantitative history's demand for generality would seem to force the historian to construct boxes before he even knows what their contents will be.

In the next few pages I hope to show that this is a false dilemma. If flexibility is built into the codebook, the historian can design codes that take account of the heterogeneity he may find among his cases, postponing the inevitable aggregating and generalizing until the data have already been read into the machine. The data on the punchcards should then be a fairly faithful mirror of the historical reality. And the reduction of these myriad individualities to a handful of broad categories can be postponed until the stage of programming, rather than being done when the codebook is designed.

The main thing to remember in designing the codes for each field is that they should be as accommodating to reality as possible. If the historian allocates a single column to a field, he may code into it up to 9 different possibilities (not counting the zero digit); for two columns, 99; for three columns, 999 different possible permutations and combinations of data. And so on. It is a false economy to think the codebook should be made as compact as possible so as to save space. The computer is indifferent to whether it reads 2 cards or 3, 15 cards or 20 for each unit. The difference to the machine is one of thousandths of a second. The difference to the researcher, on the other hand, could be enormous, since all those neat codebook categories into which he grouped his data might turn out to be the wrong ones.

Let us take an example of how it is possible to err by collapsing categories too early in the game. A historian is interested in trade flows within a country, and at the beginning of his research thinks that differences between regional economies will be critical in explaining differences in the flow of goods. So as he designs his codebook, he identifies the origin of the vehicles, or the cargo manifests, or whatever his evidence is, by region. Studying French barge manifests, he makes Flanders one point of origin, Burgundy another, Provence a third, Languedoc a fourth. The "origin of goods" field will be two columns in width, and have codes ranging from 01 to 21, to fit the 21 economic regions of France. And then, lo and behold, it turns out that interregional differences are really unimportant. Most goods perhaps change hands only in local or in international commerce. Shipments of coal from Flanders to Burgundy, say, are much less significant than shipments from one part of Flanders to another. A historian who designed his codebook in this manner would be left sitting with a pile of unintelligible data.

Far better had the researcher, in writing up the codebook, taken into consideration the variegated differences that exist in French economic reality. At least the historian should have made the basic

French administrative unit—the department—the fundamental geographic category of his research. Then if later he wished to limit himself to a regional analysis after all, he could simply have told the computer which departments are in which regions, and the computer itself would have aggregated the data to the regional level. Or better still, he could have coded the actual municipality from which the merchandise in question came, along with the department. Shortly we shall see how a series of communal codes may be devised within the brief compass of five or six columns. Being able to sort out his data by municipality would have given the historian maximum flexibility in the subsequent analysis, and at relatively little cost in the coding stage.

Thus the general principle should be followed of postponing the reduction of data to aggregate categories until as late in the project as possible. One loses nothing by taking maximum notice of detail and complexity at the coding stage, for the computer itself can easily group the data into general classes at the programming stage. It doesn't work the other way around.

One should keep in mind the second general principle of not "wasting" data. Even if the researcher does not think that certain types of information the source offers will prove important, he should nonetheless make provision for them in his codebook. The process of actually coding data—that is, writing the codes down on a special sheet so that the keypuncher may convert the rows of the sheet into IBM cards—makes adding on some extra piece of information the source may contain a simple task. As the pen races across the paper, only a marginal expenditure of effort is required to pick up additional and apparently unimportant items such as the town in which the congressman was educated or the type of carrier used to transport the French manufactures. They may turn out to be critical pieces of evidence, and if they don't, the researcher has lost little.

A related procedure to be used when feeding data from numerical sources into the computer will help the researcher check for errors. If he wishes to code data that are in tabular form in the source, he should allocate a field on the card to the total the source gives, as well as to the individual items in the total. He may be tempted to disregard the total figure reproduced in the source, on the grounds that the machine itself can total up the figures and come up with

designing the codebook

more accurate results than the clerks who labored over the table in the first place in some dismal bureau. And that it can. But the researcher will be able to spot *clerical errors* in his own coding if he later asks the computer to compare machine-totaled results against the original totals the source reported, and to print out erroneous results. If, for example, the historian is coding the occupational census returns for each American state, taking for every state the number of workers in each industrial sector, then he should build into his codebook a field entitled "total state labor force." If the computer later finds discrepancies between the total labor force it calculates, and those the source presents, then the historian will know something is wrong, possibly with the source itself, but more likely with the coding.

One final hint about techniques that avoid wastage: geographical codes should be devised with reference to official sources. The census bureau of every country already has a set of code numbers for the administrative subdivisions of the land, be they American states, English counties, French *départements*, or German *Kreise*. Rather than devising his own numbers and symbols for such districts and provinces, the historian should use the official ones. This will simplify his own task and make it possible for others to use his data, should at some future point the historian decide to deposit them in one of the new quantitative archives such as the Inter-University Consortium for Political Research in Ann Arbor for political data, or the prospective Historical Data Center at Princeton for data on collective biography.[2] In identifying municipalities, the historian should again use some official classification in which every settled place in the country is given a unique number. If such a classification is inaccessible or otherwise unsuitable, an alternate way of coding individual towns and villages is to get a gazeteer, post office handbook or other such index of localities, let the first four digits of the municipal code represent the page on which the commune appears, the last two represent the position on that page. This too

[2]Annie Kriegel, in her recent study of union growth in interwar France, had occasion to regret not using the official French numerical classification for departments. She devised one herself, unaware that any other existed, and found the ensuing analysis more cumbersome than expected. See *La croissance de la C.G.T., 1918–1921: Essai statistique* (Paris: Mouton, 1966), p. 14.

will provide a unique number for every municipality in the country.

Now we present some specific techniques for dealing with the problem of flexibility versus generality. The first is the principle of telescoping codes. Each section of tubing in the telescope represents a separate column in the field, going from the most general codes on the far left to the most refined codes on the far right. As the tubes of the glass slide out, to the right, the codes become increasingly detailed by the addition of digits. As the telescope is collapsed, the detailed codes disappear, permitting the researcher to go to a high level of generality. Another metaphor to illustrate this principle is that of the familiar high school essay outline, with its apparatus of big roman numerals, big arabic, small roman, small arabic, and so forth. The fields of a codebook should each be designed in this way when the historian is faced with the task of converting some complex event into numerals.

A few illustrations are in order. Let us say an English historian wishes to study emigration from the United Kingdom in the first part of this century. An important aspect of his project will obviously be determining the occupation of those who migrated, for significant differences between emigrants in terms of occupation could easily turn up. How does he develop a taxonomy of occupations? One idea that might strike him would be to write down on a sheet of paper as many occupations as he could think of off-hand—shoemaker, factory worker, lawyer, and such—arrange these occupations in alphabetical order, and then assign to each one a code number, going from 1 to 62, or however many he had remembered. Then more could always be added on later. Such a procedure, I feel, would be a mistake.

This *ad hoc* alphabetical listing would be flawed by a lack of both flexibility and generality. Adding on additional occupations would be an unsystematic, random procedure, likely to lead to errors of memory, omission, and duplication; hence the list would not be truly flexible. On the other hand, the job of arraying the myriad occupations into general industrial categories at the end of the research would be frustrated by the very number of those occupations. The historian would have to tell the machine to search for a basketful of codes if he wished to compare emigrants from two large sectors like textiles and metals, or from two status categories like blue-collar and white-collar.

An alternative classification of occupations would seem much more promising for this English historian's research. To start with, we'll take only the manufacturing sector of the economy, and for this broad area of occupations devise some telescoping codes. We divide the economy first into 14 major industries, into one of which every member of the manufacturing labor force must fall. The first two digits in our occupation field will be allotted to these major sectors, so that mining would be 03, textiles 07, paper and printing 11, and so on. Then we subdivide each major order into a maximum of nine sub-orders. (If one wanted more than nine, then a two-digit field, rather than a single digit, could be added on, giving the possibility of 99 codes.) The third digit in the occupational field will record the sub-order. As Figure 2–4 shows, within textiles one might have card-

Figure 2–4   How a telescoping code works: example of English occupational categories (in orders, sub-orders, and groups).

ORDER VII.   TEXTILES (0700)
   Sub-order 1.   Openers, Sorters, Blenders, Carders, Combers, Drawers (0710)
      Group 1.   Foremen, Overlookers (0711)
      Group 2.   Wool Sorters (0712)
      Group 3.   Rag and Wool Carbonisers (0713)
      Group 4.   Openers, Blenders, Rag Grinders (0714)
      Group 5.   Carders, Combers and Others (0715)
   Sub-order 2.   Spinners, Doublers (0720)
      Group 1.   Foremen, Overlookers (0721)
      Group 2.   Spinners, Piecers (0722)
      Group 3.   Doublers, Twisters, Silk Throwsters (0723)
   Sub-order 3.   Winders, Warpers, Sizers, Drawers-in (0730)
      Group 1.   Foremen, Overlookers (0731)
      Group 2.   Winders, Reelers (0732)
      Group 3.   Beamers, Warpers (0733)
      Group 4.   Sizers, Tapers, Slashers (0734)
      Group 5.   Drawers-in, Twisters-in (0735)
   Sub-order 4.   Weavers (0740)
      Group 1.   Foremen, Overlookers (0741)
      Group 2.   Weavers (not Carpets) (0742)
      Group 3.   Carpet Weavers (0743)
ORDER VIII.   TANNERS, LEATHER GOODS MAKERS (0800)
   Sub-order 1.   Leather Tanners and Dressers (0810)
      Group 1.   Foremen, Overlookers (0811)
      Group 2.   Lime and Tan Yard Workers (not Labourers) (0812)

Group 3. Curriers, Leather Dressers (0813)
Sub-order 2. Boot and Shoe Makers (0820)
   Group 1. Foremen, Overlookers (0821)
   Group 2. Boot and Shoe Makers and Repairers (not Factory) (0822)

•
•
•

ing, spinning, winding, and weaving all as separate sub-orders. Weavers, the fourth sub-order on the textile list, would be coded as 074. That doesn't mean weavers are number 74 on an alphabetical list of occupations, but that they are occupation 4 within order 070. But perhaps we desire still greater precision in our occupational classification. We wish to know exactly what kind of a weaver a worker is, whether of carpets or yard goods. So we devise a maximum of nine further groups that we may allot to each sub-order, and tack on another column to the occupational field. Carpet weaving comes third in the weaver group, so our emigrating carpet weaver will be identified as 0743 in the historian's data file.

Readers versed in English economic history will of course recognize the system of industrial categorization I have just presented as that used by the General Register Office. The English census divides the entire economy into 28 general orders, and each of them into sub-orders and groups. Only after all this elaborate apparatus do they finally resort to alphabetical listings of all skills and occupations in the modern economy.[3]

Data coded on the basis of such a system of classification are easy to manipulate. In order to discover all the emigrants in the metals industry, one need not program the machine with dozens of numbers of metal trades and product categories that our hideous alphabetical example would have thrown up. The historian need merely request the computer to treat all occupations with the first two digits of 06 as metallurgical.

Other fields could be tacked on adjacent to the occupation field for coding social status and level of qualification, whether the worker was skilled or unskilled, a supervisory person or a common laborer.

[3] The source I have used for this is Great Britain. General Register Office, *Census 1951: Classification of Occupations* (London: Her Majesty's Stationery Office, 1956), pp. 1–13.

                                                designing the codebook

The French, for example, distinguish among three separate dimensions of working life in defining a man's "occupation": first, his actual trade; second, the industrial sector in which he is employed; third, his "socio-professional status," whether a trained specialist or semi-skilled operative. These three fields together on a card would constitute a great battery of telescoping codes and allied fields, permitting literally thousands of combinations.

Data handled through this scheme of industrial classifications also acquire the advantage of comparability. Should the historian later wish to compare the results he obtained from the early twentieth century with, perhaps, those from the early nineteenth century, he has available a framework for grouping nineteenth-century occupations. And when his evidence is presented in such a standardized way, readers who themselves are studying Italy or Serbia will be able to contrast their own conclusions with his. Most nations now use similar occupational classifications, and those scholars who need to conduct research involving the coding of jobs will do themselves a disservice if they fail to have recourse to these standard taxonomies.[4]

We can apply the principle of telescoping codes to a second illustration. Charles Tilly, in his study of disturbances in modern France, has had to develop a taxonomy for the objects of crowd assaults. In his codebook he allocates two columns to the field "object of property damage," and by designing subcategories to fit within broader ones, he can in a systematic manner handle up to 99 different types of property damage. Figure 2–5 reproduces these codes in their fullest extension. The 10-series in this field might be given over to the agrarian plant: if the source reveals only that some agricultural target was assaulted without giving further information, he codes a 10 alone; if fields were attacked, 11; if farm machinery 12, if harvested crops 13, if fences and hedges 14. The 40-series is given to public facilities. Code 40 is used if exact information is lacking, 41 if a railway station, 42 if a telephone exchange, and so on up to 49, the code for "other public facilities."

[4]The basic guide to occupational classifications is the International Labour Office, *International Standard Classification of Occupations, Revised Edition, 1968* (Geneva: ILO, 1969); this handbook encompasses virtually every occupation conceivable in the mesh of five-digit codes.

Figure 2–5 How a telescoping code works: example of classifications for property damaged in riot.

CARD 83 "SCALE OF DISTURBANCE"

Columns
60–61

Objects of property damage

00 Insufficient information
01 No property damage
10 Agrarian plant
   11   Fields
   12   Harvested or stored crops
   13   Farm machinery
   14   Farm buildings
   15   Fences or hedges
   16
   17
   19   Other specific agrarian: MANDATORY COMMENT
20 Industrial plant
   21   Factory structure
   22   Machines—use comments to specify
   23   Newspaper office
   24
   29   Other specific industrial: MANDATORY COMMENT
30 Commercial plant
   31   Shop
   32   Market
   33   Cabaret or restaurant
   34   Bank
   35   Bourse
   36   Warehouse—use comments to specify
   39   Other specific commercial: MANDATORY COMMENT
40 Public facilities
   41   Train station
   42   Telephone exchange
   43   Public streets
   44   Public square
   45   Monument
   46   Meeting hall
   47   Taxation barrier
   48   Registry
   49   Other specific public facilities:
       MANDATORY COMMENT
50 Public buildings
   51   City hall

designing the codebook

        52   Palais royale
        53   Armory
        54   Episcopal palace
        55   Church
        56   Prefecture
        57   Synagogue/Temple
        58   Convent
        59   Other specific public buildings:
              MANDATORY COMMENT
    60   Residences
        61   Private house—use comments to specify
        62   Barracks
        63   Apartments
        64   Hotel
        69   Other specific residences: MANDATORY COMMENT
    70   Vehicles of transportation
        71   Automobiles
        72   Carriages
        73   Railroad cars
        74   Wagons
        75   Trucks
        76   Boats
        79   Other transport vehicles: MANDATORY COMMENT
    80   Organization headquarters
        81   Political party HQ
        82   Labor union HQ
    90   Combination of the above: MANDATORY COMMENT
    99   Objects not belonging to any of the above categories:
          MANDATORY COMMENT

Columns
62–63

Enumeration of damaged objects

State the number of objects specified in cols. 60–61 which
were the objects of attacks on property.

Insufficient information should be coded as XX.

If no objects were damaged, code 00.

Within this field Tilly may also include codes for instances that do
not exactly fit his taxonomy: 00 for insufficient information, 01 if
no property damage took place, 90 for a combination of the above,
99 for objects not belonging to any of these categories.[5] This kind

[5] I have borrowed this classification of property damage from Charles Tilly's
codebook "The General Sample of Disturbances: A Study of Urbanization and
Political Upheaval in France," University of Toronto, Department of Sociology,
draft 2–66.

of field is difficult to design, for thinking out the categories and pre-testing them with samples of data may take weeks. In the end, how-ever, such an investment of labor is repaid by the analytic precision and ease of data handling it makes possible.

Another way for the historian to protect historical complexity is to tell the machine how certain he is of the caliber of possibly un-reliable information. A special field can be placed adjacent to fields containing data of uneven quality for the purpose of saying whether the information in each case is accurate, possibly erroneous, or com-plete guesswork. Lawrence Stone employed this procedure in his study of early modern Hertfordshire manor houses. In many cases he was unsure about the exact year in which an "event," such as a fire or the building of a new wing, happened to a house. So he wrote into his codebook the field "qualification of year owner acquired house," (1 = accurate, 2 = highly probable, 3 = estimate). When the data are analyzed, Stone can instruct the machine to consider only accurate observations in some runs, and all observations—both confident and uncertain—in others.[6]

Other coding devices also exist to help free the historian from the dread of having asked the wrong questions at the beginning of his research. Here "comment cards" may be mentioned. It is clear that some potentially quantifiable historical phenomena are of such com-plexity as to defy being classified exhaustively by even the most brilliant codebook designer. The more components an historical event contains, or the longer it stretches out in time, the more numerous the forms in which the event may appear. It will, to be sure, assume a number of standard forms that the historian may anticipate in advance and design codes for. But how do we treat the anomalies?

Let us say we are studying crime in nineteenth-century New Eng-land. We are able to come up with suitable codes for the vast ma-jority of criminal acts, for they will be of a fairly predictable variety: the usual stabbings, rapes, and murders. Yet in a subject as challenging to rigorous taxonomies as crime, holes in our classifica-tion will inevitably appear. We are able to code arson, and to code theft of livestock, but what do we do about the man who sets a

[6]I am obliged to Professor Stone for permitting me to see a draft of his code-book.

designing the codebook

chicken on fire? Some symbol for "unclassifiable" is an obvious out. But if too many such unclassifiable crimes appear, we may suspect a pattern in them without having a mechanical way to identify it.

This is where comment cards come in. The codebook sets aside a couple of card numbers on which written statements will be punched in English, not in numbers. (Each letter requires one column.) In the present example, the comment that "a chicken was set on fire" would go onto the punchcard. That comment would take up only one card, but we could add more cards for longer statements. Each card would have a unique card number and common unit number as well. Later in the analysis, if a number of such unclassifiable crimes started to cluster together in an interesting way, the historian could merely ask the computer to print out the comment cards associated with those units, and so see whether some noteworthy factor lay beneath them.

Thus comment cards are another way of letting the researcher hedge his bets, postpone committing himself to general categories or specified taxonomies until the last possible moment. Other disciplines may perhaps be impatient with such procedures, suspecting that antiquarian impulses lurk behind such meticulousness about remaining true to historical reality. I would argue one reason why history has remained estranged so long from the social sciences is that historians have sensed this impatience and resented it, aware themselves of their own good reasons for following closely the minute bumps and creases in the historical record. This allegiance to the individuality of historical events goes far to explain the suspicion with which historians have viewed quantitative techniques, and especially the shibboleth of the computer. What I have done in the last few pages is to explain how historians may have their cake and eat it too, how they may allow for individuality and yet in the end achieve generality.

A last suggestion for designing codebooks is to test the document against a sampling of cases before it is made final. The historian should think of the completed codebook first as a test version; he should take it and code 50 or so cases to see how well his codes and categories hold up. Then having had the experience of actually inspecting his brainchild in the light of real data, he can return to his study, there to discard a few codes and categories that will clearly prove useless, or add on more fields and classifications to handle un-expected nuances and complexities in the source data. This is the first instance of a checking procedure that will continue all the way through to the final analysis of the output.

After all is said and done, the codebook will probably still turn out to be imperfect despite the most painstaking efforts to provide for flexibility and to collect all potentially relevant information. When the historian sits down to write up his results, new questions will almost certainly occur to him that his data leave him unable to answer, occasioning much forehead-pounding and cries of, "Why didn't I have the good sense to pick up data on tax bracket?" or some such thing. This type of inadequacy is inevitable for all code-books but those with the simplest transcription tasks. The rueful historian may console himself with the thought that if his codebook doesn't seem inadequate by the end of the project, he probably hasn't learned anything.

designing the codebook

3

Processing the Data:
Coding
and Card Handling

We have reached one of the points at which historians usually rear back in horror at sudden confrontation with an alien world. The business of designing a codebook may appear not entirely uncongenial. It can be done in the quiet of one's study, and the task of devising comprehensive, flexible codes involves an often pleasant intellectual challenge. But now we step from the book-lined study and head for the world of flashing lights in the computer center. The great grey machines lined up behind the glass, with their spinning tape drives and chattering high-speed printers, seem to symbolize renunciation of all the values and modes of investigation for which the historical profession has stood. In the foregoing chapter I tried to show, by discussing the artful design of a codebook, that the technetronic tool of the computer and the historian's craft need not necessarily be incompatible. In this chapter the historian will, as he goes from one mechanical stage of data handling to another, simply have to suppress his instinctive reaction: "Oh, my poor colonial settlers will never survive this rough treatment." As an aside, I cannot resist remarking upon a recent tendency to refer to one's file of information as a "data base." This phrase seems appropriate in the vocabulary of those who deal with "Air Force bases" and "fire bases," but it strikes me as even more out of place among humanists than most computer center argot. In general I urge: shun jargon. In specific: call the information abstracted from historical sources the "data file."

DATA CODING METHODS

If designing a codebook is the first step in computer work, the second step is coding the data. *Coding* means putting the source material into some numerical form in readiness for the third step, punching the coded data onto IBM cards. In the next few pages I shall suggest several different devices for coding. The reader may select the one that seems most appropriate to his own needs.

The usual method of coding is simply writing down the numbers on conventional data sheets, paper on which is printed a matrix 80 columns wide by perhaps 25 rows long, illustrated in the preceding chapter in Figure 2–3. The historian just sits down with his source material in front of him on one side, the data sheet on the other, and scribbles in the codes, glancing occasionally at his codebook from time to time in order to refresh his memory about some particular code. (He will quickly have his codebook memorized.) These data sheets are then delivered to the keypunch operator, who converts each row of the sheet into an IBM card.

Data sheets may be preferred to the other two coding methods I shall propose because they make possible relatively error-free card-punching. The keypunch operator, usually a young girl trained in this skill, runs her eye over each row of the data sheet without even thinking about the movements of her fingers. Data sheets accommodate this talent ideally, for their format frees the operator from worrying about anything but the data. A good keypuncher working from data sheets will make as few mistakes as one in 500.

A second coding technique is mimeographing hundreds or thousands of copies of the codebook, assigning a separate copy of the codebook to each unit, and writing in the margin the codes for that unit. Historians who are unsure of their codebook categories, or who find the men they are studying unusually difficult to classify, may prefer this method. It has the advantage of making rechecking easy, because right there next to the code is the verbal statement of what it means. Coders may also make note on the page of special circumstances that render the chosen code not entirely applicable. After the coding is finished, the historian who employs these multiple book-

lets needs but skim over them looking for earlier hedges and reservations, making final decisions about his codes. Changing one's
mind, or surveying the completed codes in immediate association
with their verbal equivalents, is more cumbersome when data sheets
are used because of the compactness of the data. If the historian is
using data sheets, he cannot scrawl all over them notations like,
"Schlunk didn't really finish his fourth term because he was institu-
tionalized as an alcoholic in 1892." With multiple codebooks such
hedges are possible, and at the last minute the researcher can easily
elect to withhold from the computer Schlunk's ill-fated fourth term.

On the other hand, multiple codebooks have some howling disadvantages. One is the great accumulation of paper they can represent. Even a simple codebook may run to three or four typewritten
pages. Only historians with complex coding problems, necessitating
long taxonomies and voluminous spreads of cards, would elect to
use such a device in the first place. In such cases they are likely to
find themselves grappling with an excess of paper as a 15-page codebook is multilithed 4000 times. Thus the sheer unwieldiness of this
mode of coding is frightening.

Multiple codebooks have a second disadvantage of increasing the
rate of error at the punching stage. The keypunch operator is con-
tinually distracted from her task by turning pages and shifting copies.
A very good operator will take this in her stride; the reliability of
even a moderately good keypuncher, however, will be frayed by the
constant need for turning from the keyboard to manipulate piles of
codebooks.

A third coding technique is keypunching the data directly from the
source. This method is most suitable for converting tabular data
into machine-readable form. Published census data, for example, are
just page after page of numbers. Going to the trouble of writing all
these down on coding sheets would appear a waste of time, for no es-
pecial coding decisions have to be made, and the operator will punch
the same numbers whether they are in the original source or in data
sheets. In this instance having a separate coding stage probably increases rather than decreases the possibility of error.[1] If codes for the
geographic units into which the census data are cross-classified are
too difficult for the keypuncher to memorize, they may be written

[1]Laurence A. Glasco proposes a way to punch manuscript census data directly from the source in "Computerizing the Manuscript Census," *Historical Methods Newsletter*, 3:1 (December, 1969), 1–4, and 3:2 (March, 1970), 20–25.

in the margin of the Xerox copy of the source. Direct keypunching has the advantage of saving time and money for coding; it has the disadvantage of marginally increasing the distractions to the keypuncher.

One tip: When punching from the source, try to make all fields the same number of columns wide. The keypuncher is then less likely to become confused about how many columns are allocated to which fields, or about where one field begins and another field ends. This will reduce the error rate.

A variation of punching from the source is to take the data directly from one's note cards onto IBM cards. If the coding scheme is simple, one may just write on lined index cards the material one reads from the archival source, or newspapers, or whatnot. Each line on the index card represents a separate field, and the keypuncher need simply run her eye down the card, punching the contents of each line in its allotted place on the IBM card. Theodore Rabb used this technique in doing research on investors in English seaborne commerce. A typical card from his note box would have appeared thus:

> JONES, THOS.
> 8453
> 523
> — [when the field is blank]
> W8CL4
> 043
> 7
>
> —

The keypuncher quickly memorizes the codebook format, knowing that the punches on the second line go in columns 6 to 9 of the IBM card, those on the third line in 10 to 12, and so on through the entire file card. She has merely to flip through the note cards the researcher assembled in the English document rooms, and presto! his entire file is ready for machine processing.[2]

CHECKING FOR ERRORS

Whatever coding technique is selected, the historian should do some checking before he passes from coding to keypunching. Mis-

[2] I am grateful to Professor Rabb for providing me with this example in a letter.

takes can creep into this kind of research so easily. A moment of in-attention and the data in a certain field are entered in one column too far to the right; a brief spell of daydreaming and one page in the source is coded twice; the coding is interrupted for a coffee break and four South Carolina preachers are omitted from the file; as the research assistant's fingers tire, his fives begin to look like threes, his nines like sevens. It is absolutely essential to devise some procedure for systematically checking for such mistakes.

I would recommend check coding a certain percentage of the original cases, perhaps one in 50 or one in 100. Then compare the recodes to the originals; if only random errors emerge, fine. One cannot do much about isolated mistakes, such as misreading a num-ber occasionally, which seem to result more from acts of God than from anything else. If the coder has been too sloppy about such ran-dom errors, then the researcher will have to give some thought to having the job done over again. (To avert that kind of calamity, check coding should commence before a large coding job is very far advanced.) But if the recoding reveals that the errors fall in a pattern—a tendency to miss the next to the last column on the source page, an occasional transposing of two fields—the errors can be hunted down and corrected. Again, I emphasize the need for a careful checking of the data sheets. Few things are more frustrating in computer research than having to throw away finished output and run programs again because at some late date coding errors are discovered. (*Output* is what comes out of the computer on special printed forms.)

In addition to clerical coding errors, discrepancies in interpretation of the source data may arise to plague the researcher. When one is coding qualitative data—descriptions of the sequence of military actions, for example, or the stated causes of suicide cases—one coder may differ from another on how some nonstandardized phenomenon is to be evaluated. One of the research assistants of a military his-torian may see the maneuver of a tank battalion simply as code 1221 (armored flanking maneuver); another assistant may interpret the same maneuver as code 1224 (effort to mount armored pincer). Thus the historian ends up with two different codes for the same historical phenomenon. One coder has simply thought of a maneuver differently from another coder.

Several steps may be taken to counter this variety of interpretive error. As a prophylactic measure, the codebook should contain very strict and detailed coding instructions, devised on the basis of extensive test coding, on how to describe in a standard way events which the source relates in a nonstandard manner. If the same person is doing all the coding, he should occasionally review the decisions he has taken in earlier cases, so that almost imperceptible interpretive drifts may be halted. Over the weeks, for example, the historian ceases to think of riparian disputes as code 62 (boundary conflicts over *water* rights), and conceives them instead as code 68 (boundary conflicts over *navigation* rights). If the historian has employed research assistants to do the coding, he should bring them together for regular meetings, discuss problem cases, and have them recode one another's work from time to time. Or better yet, have the assistants do their work sitting together around a table, where they may constantly compare decisions and discuss problems.

A more sophisticated way of stopping discrepancies in coding is through a computer check. If the codebook is quite complex, and the cases numerous, the historian may ask the computer to compare coded units against recodes of the same units, and print out fields where discrepant codes exist. The originals may then be patched up. Here a caveat: such programming can become expensive and time-consuming. If it is at all possible to spot inconsistencies manually rather than by machine, such discrepancy programming should be avoided.

In conclusion I wish to emphasize that the coding is the core of a computer-aided project. The machine can process only what it has been told, and mistakes in coding mean supplying the machine with misinformation. Most historians who use computers will have selected this tool because they wish to analyze a large number of potentially complex events. Many of these events will be retailed in verbal, not in numerical, form in the sources. Coding decisions taken in the course of numerically standardizing these diverse, non-uniform accounts and events will thus be of crucial importance. Keep in mind that when the historian lets the coding of such events out of his hands, he is letting go of his entire research project. The historian must know exactly what his codes mean, what he thought they meant two weeks ago, and what his research assistants think they mean. To blunder here is to feed garbage into the machine. And as computer people say, "garbage in, garbage out."

Once the coding is out of the way, we arrive at the stage of producing cards (keypunching) and manipulating them in various ways
(card handling). The information I am about to purvey is purely
mechanical, entirely devoid of intellectual substance, yet indispen-
sible in computer work.

The first problem that arises in keypunching is whether the historian himself should do the work, and save money, or hire a professional keypuncher. Learning to keypunch is no more difficult than
learning to type. The keyboards on a keypunch machine and a typewriter are similar, and feeding cards through the machine is no more
difficult than feeding paper into a typewriter. Should the historian
wish to do so, he could easily learn to operate the keypunch and
produce his own cards. It is in fact desirable for him to familiarize
himself with the machine so that he can perform such simple feats as
reproducing damaged cards, typing out "control cards" for programs,
and the like.

Nevertheless, the historian is best advised to hire a professional
keypuncher to turn his data sheets into punched cards. Just as a
man would not learn how to type from scratch in order to produce
an article for a journal, neither would he learn keypunching in order
to do computer work. The professionals are trained to work quickly
and accurately; they charge no more by the hour than do secretaries
or stenographers; and they give the researcher the confidence that
his data are right. A good keypuncher can turn out 100 cards an hour,
and at that rate all but the largest "decks" can be done in a matter
of days. The expense is negligible, the returns impressive. The personnel of the computer center will doubtlessly be able to recommend
to him a qualified keypuncher.

With keypunching, as with all other stages of computer research,
a checking procedure is necessary. The historian will want to determine whether systematic errors were made in the punching. Machines called *card verifiers* are available for this purpose. The historian himself, or a second keypuncher, repunches every fiftieth card
or so on the verifier, feeding into it the original card, and watching
for a notch to appear on the top edge of the card if the number he
punches is different from the number already punched on the card.

A word of warning about keypunch machines. Just as there are different generations of computers, there are different generations of keypunches. IBM's model 026, a dull grey machine, dominated the market for a long time, until IBM brought out the newer 029, pictured in Figure 3–1, a jazzier looking device with blue keys and

Figure 3–1   The 029 keypunch (courtesy of IBM).

lots of shiny plastic. The punches both machines yield are exactly the same, *except for a couple of the punctuation marks,* such as the equals sign and the parentheses. Researchers who plan to use punctuation symbols as codes must be sure that their card punching is done on one or other of the machines alone. Also, keep in mind that programs for the IBM 360 computer should be punched on the 029. These potential problems will vanish as the 026s are taken out of circulation.

Without warning, I have insinuated the reader into the machine room. This is where the keypunches are kept, and where the historian will find most of the pieces of machinery—technically called unit record equipment—I am about to mention. All computer centers have a machine room, often referred to as a consulting or editing room, and remote access terminals as well will probably have some card handling machinery.

The historian takes his freshly minted IBM cards from the keypunch to other pieces of equipment in the machine room. Before we introduce these, a housekeeping detail about the physical handling of cards should be dispatched. Just before the user places the deck in any of the various hoppers, he must square them up, which means aligning them neatly in a pack so that neither vertical nor horizontal edges protrude. A messy deck with cards sticking out is highly vulnerable to creasing and notching, undesirable because imperfect cards jam in the machinery, slowing down operations or actually causing the cards to be mutilated beyond recovery. All equipment in the machine room has joggle blocks attached, little platforms with vertical right angles against which the cards are plumped and pounded until all are perfectly aligned. Once the edges have been tapped smooth, the cards should be fanned once, to remove the static electricity, before being placed in the machinery. A final housekeeping detail: the cards should be stored packed tightly together so as to prevent warping, and in a dry room for the same reason.

The first device the historian encounters in the machine room is the accounting machine, on which he will "list" his cards. Listing is both a noun and a verb, the activity he does at this machine and the paper that emerges from it with an exact reproduction of his data deck. The codes of each card are printed on a different line of the listing. The researcher needs this sheet of paper for two reasons. One, a listing is an easy way to catch punching mistakes. In fact, a good keypuncher will list the cards and check them over herself before she even surrenders the job to the historian. As the researcher looks over the listing of his data himself, he will try to find "justification" errors, that is, punches in the wrong field. A common mistake is entering a punch in the wrong column by one. Punches that are a space too far to the right of the field will stick out like a sore thumb on the listing. Also, the user may catch units accidentally omitted or duplicated by scanning the listing. If he is working with, say, German counties numbered from 01 to 50, and the listing shows two 36s but no 37, it is clear a mistake has been made.[3]

A listing is also important because it is the most convenient guide to the data. Does the programmer wish to know if a certain code is used? The listing is consulted. If the historian wishes to refresh his memory quickly about the year in which data for a certain field are missing, he checks the listing. A "wild score" appears in the output: four foster homes in the town of Kirchenlamitz supported eight million orphaned children in 1840? Check the listing to see first what figure the computer read, then determine if a programming, a punching, a coding, or a source error was made. The listing is a key means of controlling one's data. Lists that are more than a few pages long should be placed in the stiff-cover binders available for preserving computer output.

Another piece of equipment in the machine room is the reproducing punch. Before the historian proceeds to further operations with his cards, he should copy the deck on this device. Now, some important advice: Always keep a master duplicate of the data file in some safe place. The coffee rooms in computer centers are legion with tales of lost data: Someone's cards disappeared from the file drawer; the computer operators lost someone's data deck; the operators "clobbered" the tape that was the sole record of someone's data. (In computer talk, mistakenly having the computer write on a data tape, whereby the data existing on the tape are erased, is called *clobbering*. Despite abundant safeguards, such as stipulating that tapes without a little plastic ring in the center may under no circumstances be written on, clobbering is a frequent type of oper-

[3]This point about listing to catch justification errors may influence the design of some codebooks. When drawing up multicard codebooks for data that are already numerical in the source, keep the data fields the same number of columns wide. This will facilitate error checking; and the researcher can spot justification errors by looking at the listing of the whole deck, sparing himself the trouble of sorting all the card ones into one pile, the card twos into another, and so on.

In some computer centers an accounting machine is not present because the computer itself will list the cards. The reader will have to inquire about exactly what arrangement prevails in the center he wishes to use.

ator error.) Reproducing punches serve purposes other than supplying reserve decks. Let us say the historian wishes to shift a field
from one group of columns to another for some reason. The computer itself can of course do this, but often a simpler way is to wire
a board in the reproducing punch to transfer the holes from one
column to another. A winning smile will persuade some lounging
graduate student to abandon his Coke bottle long enough to demonstrate how all this is done.

Many installations are outfitted with a further piece of equipment:
an interpreter. Although the cards that emerge from keypunches
have the number in each column printed at the top (*interpreted*),
those that the computer or the reproducing punch emit do not. Interpreted cards are much easier to use than uninterpreted ones, because the historian does not have to squint carefully at the actual
punches on the card to determine its contents, but only to glance
at the top of the card. In the absence of a card interpreter, one may
print the punches on a deck by running the cards through a keypunch machine that has been specially outfitted with an interpret
device. Either a card interpreter or an interpreting keypunch should
be on hand at every installation.

A final piece of equipment in the machine room is the *card sorter*.
This device takes a deck of cards and distributes each card in one
of 13 pockets, depending on which punch is entered in the column
of the card one is "sorting on." Ten of the pockets are for the 10
numerical punching positions, from zero to nine, two are for the 11
and 12 zone punches at the top of the card, one pocket is for columns
with no punch in them. The reader will think back to all the FBI
movies he has seen in which the G-men are hunting a killer, and
to the sound of dramatic background music punchcards are seen
flipping through the air. This is a card sorter, picking out suspects
on the basis of their physical characteristics, method of operation, or
other information punched on the card. A variant of this machine is
called the *counter-sorter*, for it counts electrically the number of
cards that are sorted into each pocket, telling the user how often
each code in the field was used.

The card sorter is used mainly in order to arrange the data deck
into some rational order as an aid to programming. The sorter first
separates the cards into a number of grand categories, and then
within each category into some sub-order. The student of the thou-

sand congressmen in the last chapter would, for example, arrange his cards on the basis of the year in which each man began his tenure; then within that year subarrange them by political party. One of the first things the programmer will ask the researcher is, "How are the cards sorted?" Knowing about this requirement beforehand will prevent the embarrassment of having to reply "Huh?" or "Wha' dat?"

Several other pieces of card handling equipment are occasionally found in the machine room, notably the collator and the electronic statistical machine. Collators are designed to compare fields of data in two separate groups of cards, statistical machines to combine the counting and sorting functions of the other, previously mentioned devices. I will spare the reader a detailed discussion of them, partly because they are rarely found in university facilities, as Kenneth Janda explains, "because computing centers are organized and run largely for physical scientists" who require such equipment infrequently,[4] but also partly because efficiency is served in the long run by the use of computers rather than these machines to analyze data.

In the past these card handling machines have often been used as analytic tools. Some of the projects cited in Chapter 1 depended on card sorters rather than computers. The card sorter, and especially the counter-sorter, serves analysis because it tells the user the frequency of each code in each field. If the historian wants to know how southern congressmen voted on Taft-Hartley, he first lets the sorter separate out of the main data deck those congressmen who were from the South; he then takes this pile and sorts on the Taft-Hartley column (1 = yes; 2 = no); he then counts the number of cards to drop into the 1 pocket and the 2 pocket to get his answer. Yet compared to the computer, the card counter-sorter and statistical machine are primitive tools, cumbersome to use and lacking in flexibility. They have no memories, and can do only one job at a time. Their worst feature is that they encourage the researcher to squeeze his data onto a single 80-column IBM card, forcing him to aggregate and reduce his information at the coding rather than the processing stage. In the chapter on codebook design we saw why premature data reduction was to be avoided. But counter-sorters encourage just this kind of sacrifice and truncation of information because they

[4]*Data Processing: Applications to Political Research* (Evanston, Ill.: Northwestern University Press, 1965), p. 80.

make unwieldy the use of any data format other than single-column fields and single-card units. My feeling is that historians should avoid the beguiling simplicity of card sorters in their analyses of data. Scholars who wish to go beyond the simplest tabulations will find that the computer repays in the long run the extra investment of time, money, and energy it requires.

A final point about using the machine room. The historian should never hesitate to seek advice from the computer center people themselves. My descriptions of many of these mechanisms are cursory, and the reader will remain in the dark as to how they actually operate. When he appears in the machine room, deck of cards in hand, he will have to ask someone to show him how to activate the accounting machines and counter-sorters. Beyond this mechanical instructional level, the user will have all kinds of other questions, many of which will surface in the next chapter, about the availability of "canned" programs or of "line-overrides" for printing large amounts of output in the same job. He will have to turn to the staff of the computer center for assistance. In most cases a welcoming reception will await him. The director of the center will in all likelihood prove exceedingly cordial and make special efforts to help the novice.

All this friendliness is not necessarily due to a basic generosity of spirit among the staff, although that too may be present. Rather it results from the imperialist spirit of computer personnel. They wish to enlarge their own empires and usefulness by seeking converts, and historians are notorious in these circles as an unreconstructed group. It also results from the center's desire to seek a counterweight to the natural and applied sciences, which everywhere monopolize the facilities. The center's staff may free themselves from the yoke of the physicists and electrical engineers by pointing to hordes of historians descending upon the facility clamoring for service. For these reasons, then, the historian should not be timid about enlisting aid from the upper echelons of the center. Support from the director will also make it easier for him to cope with the sullenness of the operators and clerks he will doubtless encounter at the lower echelons.

4

Processing the Data:
The Computer and
Programming

The principal sticking point in computer research is the computer itself. Those who enjoy the challenge of designing codebooks, who easily master card handling techniques, often draw up short at actually processing data with a computer because the veil of mystery over the subject is so frightening. It has been noised about that using computers has something to do with programming, and that programming in turn involves learning recondite languages with names like FORTRAN and COBOL. All this seems like so much effort, like such a wrenching departure from accustomed modes of investigation, that in the eyes of most historians the computer takes on the appearance of the Wizard in the Land of Oz. Now it is true that historians will encounter certain problems in working with a computer. These will have to be faced head on. But the purpose of this chapter is to show that the amount of retooling required will be modest, and that the computer is no more mysterious than the automobile engine once one understands what is involved. The next few pages will explain what computers are, how they work, and what differences exist among them. I shall take pains to introduce the reader to the arcane vocabulary of computer specialists. Finally, I will make a couple of suggestions on how the tangled problem of programming may best be unraveled.

COMPUTERS: HOW THEY WORK

The initial confusion many historians feel when encountering the world of computers for the first time is caused by the names and series numbers of the machines themselves. Let us talk a little about the different computers the reader is likely to meet. In all likelihood they will be manufactured either by IBM, the Control Data Corporation, or the Digital Equipment Corporation. IBM dominates the market, supplying equipment to the vast majority of the 529 American colleges and universities that used computers in 1967–1968. Of these 1559 computers, 95 per cent were manufactured by IBM. This staggering preponderance is slightly reduced because a firm like Control Data may supply the main processors (an alternate term for computer) at many institutions, while IBM supplies the auxiliary equipment and the smaller computers used by research institutes and the administration.

There are three different kinds of IBM computers to keep track of: a "second generation" of large computers bearing numbers in the 7000s; a second generation of small computers numbered in the 1000s; and a third generation of large and small computers whose serial numbers all begin with 360. The older second generation machines were the first computers made with transistor components, replacing the ancient vacuum-tube machines of the first generation. Among the most popular of the large-scale processors were the IBM 7040 and 7094; of the latter 26 were still in operation in 1967–1968. I mention this machine particularly because we shall shortly hear more about it in connection with a ready-made set of programs called DATA-TEXT. The second generation 7000 machines, some 85 in number at present, are now being replaced by the third generation. Six hundred and thirty of these new IBM system 360 computers currently exist in colleges and universities, popular medium-scale models being the 360/40 and the 360/50, and a favored large-scale processor the 360/65. These models differ from one another in their capacity to store data and in the speed with which they operate. Users at institutions with the small-scale IBM 1000 series may be slightly at a disadvantage if they wish to process large data files. Aside from that, which computer the institution has is of secondary concern to the average user.[1]

A few words about how computer systems work are in order. Computer people talk about the *system* rather than the *machine* or the *computer* because a computer system is a composite of interrelated subsystems of controls. To start with, every computer has a network of controls that acts as a traffic monitor, making sure jobs are being read in properly and that the printing out of each in rapid order goes well. This is no mean feat, for the 360s are designed to handle hundreds of jobs in an hour, processing each in seconds. This monitor system is called the *operating system* ("OS") in the IBM 360 series. Within this general monitor system, which supervises all the different jobs the great 360 is simultaneously doing, is a subsystem called the *input-output* system ("I/O" for short). This governs specifically the reading in and printing out of jobs. Figure 4–1 shows how the various systems of the computer interrelate.[2]

Instructions that guide the computer's subsystems are called "software," which simply means the programs that are built right into the computer. The physical accoutrements of the machine itself are known as "hardware." The essential computer hardware is its memory cells, tiny two-place switches that record data by storing a 0 or 1. With these little switches the computer can retain in its memory all possible combinations of letters and numbers. The computer people call these little switches *bits*, and in the IBM 360 series eight of them together register a computer character, or *byte*.

The number of bytes a machine has is important because they

[1]Information on university computing systems is conveniently summarized in Frank H. Gille, ed., *Computer Yearbook and Directory*, 2nd ed. (Detroit: American Data Processing, 1968), pp. 830–907; the facts cited above were taken from pp. 830–32. Which computer the institution has is in fact of importance in determining the availablity of packaged programs, which are written for particular systems and are often not transferable. Yet canned programs abound in such number that suitable subroutines (as the clusters of instructions in packaged programs are sometimes called) are sure to exist in computer centers for the basic statistical requirements a historian is likely to have.

[2]Taken from Donald J. Veldman, *Fortran Programming for the Behavioral Sciences* (New York: Holt, Rinehart & Winston, Inc., 1967), p. 3.

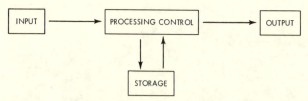

Figure 4–1   Interrelationship between various computer systems.

determine its storage capacity. Many kinds of programs, and many kinds of research projects as well, require a certain minimum of storage for their successful execution. Because the amount of core storage varies from computer to computer, the historian should inquire about the size of the memory in his particular installation. Memory is frequently measured in units of approximately one thousand bytes, denoted by a K. (To be exact, K is 1024 bytes, not 1000 bytes, for reasons too complicated to go into.) The IBM 360/65, for example, is a machine with a minimum of 500 K.

Figure 4–2 illustrates the various pieces of hardware that together constitute a computer system. In the foreground are the central processing unit and main storage, the front part of which is the console. The typewriter is used to give instructions to the system and receive messages from it. The other pieces of equipment are devices for either reading data into core storage (*input*) or for getting results out (*output*). Not shown is a *card read punch*, which both accepts IBM cards for processing and punches out new decks (*punched output*). Nor are the input-output devices called *disk drives* depicted —a matter we shall shortly take up. In the center rear are the system's *tape drives*, devices that read magnetic data off tapes or create new tapes as output. To the right rear is a high-speed printer whence comes printed output on paper forms.

PROGRAMMING AND PROGRAMMING LANGUAGES

These pieces of hardware serve to either read in data, perform calculations, or produce output in one of its various forms (print, tape, disk). Getting them to do their stuff is called programming.

Figure 4–2 The IBM System 360 computer (courtesy of IBM).

Because the few simple programming terms have always loomed so
menacingly in the eyes of historians contemplating computer research, I should explain a little about programming languages, and
how a programmer goes about his work. Again, the historian does
not absolutely need to know any of this in order to do computer
work; but it helps to dispel the aura of mystery that surrounds the
machine and to give the researcher a surer grasp of the technique.

Programming involves two basic steps: distributing the input data
among different parts of core storage, and specifying the operations
to be performed upon the data. In order to carry out this agenda,
the programmer writes a series of statements, some of them close
to real language, in a *source* or *program* language. Within the computer a package of software programs called the *compiler* converts
the instructions written in this source language to another language
comprehensible to the machine itself, called *object* or *machine* lan-

guage. These newly translated program instructions then go through the control unit, which is the hardware with all the blinking lights, and actually direct the execution of the job.

What are some of these program languages called and which are most suitable for the needs of historians? There are two major languages—FORTRAN and COBOL—that may be used on most computers, whether manufactured by IBM or not. FORTRAN stands for *FOR*mula *TRAN*slation, COBOL for *CO*mmon *B*usiness *O*riented *L*anguage. Other languages are more restricted in their application: ALGOL, which stands for *ALGO*rithmic *L*anguage, is used heavily in Europe; PL/1, which is fast becoming a general-purpose language, is available mainly for IBM machines. COBOL is the language many historians may prefer to work in because its expressions are closer to English than the mathematical FORTRAN phrases. FORTRAN, on the other hand, has the advantage of requiring less fussiness in writing and is less loquacious than COBOL, compressing into a single instruction messages that COBOL requires four or five statements to get across. Also, FORTRAN is much more suited than COBOL to statistics, and most packaged programs of statistics in computer center libraries are written in it, few in COBOL.

How does a programmer actually manipulate the computer? His main task is to assign various sections of the computer's storage area to different fields of the codebook, and in feeding data into the machine to make sure that all the separate codes get neatly filed away in their various "addresses." If one likens the core storage to a large cavern, to be filled by the historian's data deck, the programmer's job is to assign the far upper left-hand corner to one kind of table, the upper right-hand corner to another, and so on until the programmer has created in the machine's memory the matrices of all the tables he wishes the machine to produce.

This process will become clearer with an illustration. Let us say the historian wants from the computer a table that will cross-classify the American industrial labor force by state and by industry. He envisions a table 11 columns across, for each of 11 major industries, and 50 rows long, for each of the 50 states. In order to make this kind of table, the computer programmer creates in the storage area of the machine the exact duplicate of this table, called a two-dimensional *array*, with 11 columns and 50 rows. Then as the data cards come into the computer, the programmer asks the machine to inspect the fields that contain the relevant information. The machine comes across an Arkansas card. Into the Arkansas row (number 2) goes hurtling the industrial labor force of that state. And each piece of Arkansas information comes to rest in the proper industrial column: Arkansas' metallurgical workers halt in column 2 of row 2, her service employees in column 9 of row 2, and so forth. Once this table is created in the mind of the machine, the programmer has only to ask the computer to regurgitate it onto paper, along with the numerous other tables, such as those cross-classifying labor force by age, or labor force by skill level, which he simultaneously has fashioned in the storage area. That, with a few refinements, is the essence of programming.

After the programmer has written his program, full of instructions like MOVE DATA TO ARRAY (N,J), he *compiles* it, which is to say he submits it to a computer subsystem called the compiler. The compiler checks over the program for syntactical errors like putting the wrong punctuation mark after an instruction, and then converts the user's program into machine language (source langauge into object language) that the computer can understand. After the program has been correctly compiled, it is ready to actually supervise the input of the data and to direct the execution of calculations. I mention this so the historian will know what is happening when he asks his programmer how the job is coming and gets back the reply, "It's still being compiled."

Veteran programmers will bridle at my assertion that the putting out of a few cross-tabulations is the core of their profession. Let me hasten to add that programming requirements within the social sciences go to vastly more sophisticated levels than just cross-classification of data. For example, historians who have numerical information on a large number of characteristics of the population they are studying will want to make use of advanced statistical techniques, to be described later under the category of "multiple regression." The programming of these statistics is quite complex, for it involves instructing the computer to solve a number of simultaneous algebraic equations. The point is that the historian's needs may well go beyond the simple cross-tabulating of data I chose as an example.

Once the program is written, the next problem is how shall the data be fed into the machine, what type of "input" is most appropriate. There are three different kinds of input, each suitable to a different kind of data file: *card, tape,* and *disk. Card input* is the placement of the historian's IBM cards themselves in the machine's hopper. Historians with small data files of a thousand cards or so may prefer the simplicity of card input, which permits easy rearrangement of the deck, adding to or subtracting from it simply by shuffling the cards about, and easy error correction. The disadvantage of card input is that when large files are involved the machine reads the cards slowly (the hopper's examination of single cards being a relatively tedious process). The cards themselves do not always survive the hazards of the computer center, and tales of decks separated by negligent operators, or of misplaced files and missing cards, are commonplace. A final disadvantage of card input is that after a number of passes through the hopper or the sorter the deck becomes frayed, starts to jam up the machinery, and has to be replaced.

Once the historian has his data file in order, he will probably prefer to put it on a *computer tape,* the second form of input, for general ease of handling. The operators can manipulate tapes rapidly and efficiently (in contrast to card files, which are prone to go crashing to the floor in disarray). Moreover, the tapes are rarely lost, and the data on them never mixed up. In the case of even middle-sized files (more than a couple of card boxes), tapes spare the historian the cumbersome transporting of the cards to and fro between office and computer center. Finally, should it be necessary to change the data on the tape, adding new information or correcting old, simple computer routines can handle this "updating."

The third kind of computer input is the *disk* (called *direct access storage device,* or DASD). The disk is like an extension of the computer's memory in which one's data are permanently filed. A disk (part of a *disk pack*) looks like a stack of phonograph records in a glass case. The historian will derive two advantages from filing his data in a disk. For one thing, the disk rushes its contents into the computer's memory much faster than tapes or cards, resulting in important savings of computer time. For another, disk data may be *randomly accessed*, meaning that information anywhere on the disk can be instantly shot into the computer's storage area, in contrast to tape, which forces the machine to read all previous records before it comes to the desired ones.[3]

COMPUTER TIME

A final technical consideration is the question of computer time. All computer centers charge by the hour for the use of their central processor, starting at around $200 for academic users and going to upwards of $600 an hour for commercial ones. Even though within the university community money may never change hands, computer centers must budget users, whether individuals or departments, to fixed amounts of time. As the historian will be competing with other scholars for access to the computer, he should have some idea what his time requirements will be and how such things are estimated.

Estimating one's time requirements for the third generation machines is difficult because several factors enter into the actual cost of a job. Paying for computer use is much more complicated than simply keeping track of the chronological time to have elapsed while the computer was reading in and processing the job. The user will be charged at one rate for "compiling" time, that is, for the period in which his source program is being converted into an object program. He may be charged at another rate for each unit of input to go into core storage. He may be charged at a third rate for the "printing" time consumed, which means the time it takes the machine to instruct a tape or disk within the system what to print. He will not have to pay for the actual time the printer spends putting output onto paper. Some computer centers, however, make a separate charge for each line of output. The upshot of all this is that the historian will be unable to calculate his time requirements very

[3]A fourth kind of input used by historians and social scientists in the past is perforated paper tape. It owes its existence to the relative inexpensiveness of tape punches compared to card punches. Paper tape is frustrating to use because of the difficulty in reading and correcting it. Cards are preferable in every regard, and paper tape should be viewed as an expedient forced upon the user by miserly institutions.

closely. Prudence alone, therefore, dictates that historians with big input files and expectations of reams of output had best prepare to wrest a substantial amount of time from the computer center.

But how much time? Because exact time requirements will be a function of the size of the file, the program language selected, the amount of computation involved, and the kind of computer being used, I can give the reader a rough sense of his needs only through examples. Quite a small job, for instance, would be one involving perhaps 6000 cards (three boxes) on which some simple calculations were to be performed and from which a few modest pages of output would flow. If the program were written in COBOL, the IBM 360/65 would take about a minute to do this job. Let me illustrate the time needed for a very large job, on the other hand, with an example from my own research on strikes. My programmer was attempting to read in several files simultaneously in order to compute some strike rates. The input was some 40,000 cards, each representing a separate strike, which had been put onto tape. These 40,000 records occupied three tapes. A further input file was 8300 labor force records on a separate tape. It took the computer over 16 minutes—a huge amout of time—to read in all these records and to calculate a figure for each industry in each department of France in every year between 1890 and 1935: the number of strikers per 100,000 members of the labor force.

These examples give us a very approximate idea of how long individual jobs might take. How about entire research projects? Returning to the little job involving three boxes of cards, let us assume that 15 separate submissions will be necessary for the programmer to "debug" his routines and get everything executing properly, for the historian to look at the first output and send it back for emendations and corrections, and for the final production runs, incorporating all the new ideas the historian has thought of since he first started getting output, to be carried out. So that's 15 runs; we multiply one minute per run times 15 and get an estimated project time of around a quarter of an hour. Right? Wrong. The last rule of thumb to keep in mind when estimating time is that the historian will need at least twice as much time as he thinks he'll need. And to be on the safe side, ask for three times as much. In computer research, the historian's intellectual curiosity inevitably outpaces his original interest, necessitating further data processing. Also, the beguiling simplicity of the ideal computer study, such as it is presented here, will most certainly be belied by the complexities of harsh reality, by blunders and false starts, by too-short line estimates and missing control cards. All this will take additional computer time.

THE PROGRAMMING DILEMMA

Now we have reached the question of who does the programming. Here is the single rough spot in computer work, for although the historian himself will be able to handle all phases of the analysis up to programming, he will in all likelihood be unable to write the programs. He will have to hire somebody, spend money, for a brief moment entrust the fate of his research to another. I despair at having to offer this counsel; yet there is no way to avoid it (aside from a few gleams of hope I shall present at the end of the discussion).

Let us consider the alternatives. Learning to program on one's own is not an impossibility. The main dimensions of programming are understanding the logic a computer will accept and learning the symbols that execute the job. The historian would have to invest perhaps two weeks of hard work in acquiring the very basics of FORTRAN or COBOL. Then a laborious period of trial and error would be necessary before one could write programs at all competently. Finally, the historian who wished to embark upon this brave course would have to learn the particular operating system at his institution, since systems vary from one university to another. The IBM 360 particularly requires direction through several *job control cards*: Are the data on cards, tape, or disk? Is the input "labeled?" Is the system supposed to compile, compute, or "dump?"

If the researcher resolves to press on through this thicket of difficulties the best way to learn programming is to sit down with a COBOL manual (the language nonstatistical historians will prefer to FORTRAN) and start to read it.[4] Experienced programmers ad-

---

[4]The first thing to read in self-teaching should be a general introduction to computers and programming. Appropriate are Jessica Hellwig's brief guide, *Introduction to Computers and Programming* (New York: Columbia University

vise against enrolling in one of the gaudy programming schools now flourishing like pizza parlors. Rather, the historian should complement his study of the manual with visits to the special intensive courses in programming most computer centers offer. My own feeling is that the investment of time and effort in all this is not worth it. Programming can eat up days better devoted to reflection and research. The debugging of programs can be an ulcerating business, as one goes back over the logic and the syntax of the program time and again, endeavoring to discover why it doesn't work.[5]

Hiring a programmer is the alternative I would recommend to most researchers. Many graduate departments in the social sciences —geography, sociology, political science, economics—now teach computer programming to their students as a matter of course, and often to advanced undergraduates. Nowadays virtually every graduate student in disciplines that are empirically oriented, such as psychology departments given heavily to experimental studies, will be able to write elementary computer programs. Thus there is a plethora of talent around the universities. (Indeed, sometimes one is moved to think that all graduate students except those in history

---

Press, 1969); the initial four chapters (pp. 1–86) of Veldman, *Fortran Programming for the Behavioral Sciences*; or the first five chapters (pp. 1–213) of Theodor D. Sterling and Seymour V. Pollack, *Introduction to Statistical Data Processing* (Englewood Cliffs, N.J.: Prentice-Hall, Inc., 1968); or finally the admirable but now somewhat dated book by Bert F. Green, Jr., *Digital Computers in Research: An Introduction for Behavioral and Social Scientists* (New York: McGraw-Hill Book Company, 1963). Then the historian may turn to one of the programming manuals themselves for detailed instruction. To be recommended among these are Donald Dimitry and Thomas Mott, Jr., *Introduction to Fortran IV Programming* (New York: Holt, Rinehart & Winston, Inc., 1966); Daniel D. McCracken, *A Guide to FORTRAN IV Programming* (New York: John Wiley & Sons, Inc., 1965); and the string of McCracken manuals on ALGOL, COBOL, the IBM 1601, the IBM 1401, and so forth, all published by Wiley. Clarence B. Germain's *Programming the IBM 360* (Englewood Cliffs, N.J.: Prentice-Hall, Inc., 1967) is both an instructional manual on the system and an introduction to the languages PL/1, FORTRAN, COBOL, and Assembly Language, but the immersion it offers is sudden and quick, like an ice-cold bath.

[5]Janda advises political scientists to acquire at least a rudimentary knowledge of computer programming so as to better understand the capabilities of the machine, to communicate with their programmers more effectively, and to become aware of analytic approaches they otherwise might not have thought of. Historians may in my opinion disregard this advice because the questions they will need to ask the computer are normally so straightforward that a knowledge of programming would contribute little to their ability to formulate them. See *Data Processing: Applications to Political Research* (Evanston, Ill.: Northwestern University Press, 1965), pp. 105–6.

and fine arts know some statistics and programming.) Programmers with a social science background are preferable to those whose computer training lies in the natural or applied sciences. They are more familiar with the questions the historian will want to ask, and will also be able to suggest ways of answering those questions that may not have occurred to the historian himself.

So this is one course of action—consult the bulletin board at the computer center, or call upon colleagues in the sociology department to recommend a competent student, or wander into the machine room and inquire if anyone wants a job. The programming of such short, simple jobs as many historians will have should not take more than a week or so of part-time labor. Scribble a few notations down; punch them up on control cards; compile the program; debug it; run the data; submit the output to the historian, who will probably suggest a few revisions in the presentation of the tables; resubmit; and cash in the payroll check. This assumes, as the most elementary of all possible programming scenarios, that the historian will not want the machine to do any preliminary manipulation of the data, such as combining cases or bunching fields together. It also assumes that the historian has been sufficiently clear-sighted to know exactly the kind of output he wished to see in advance, and that his intellectual curiosity was not stimulated by the first results to propose new kinds of tabulations that hitherto had not occurred to him. These two preconditions of the simplest possible programming job will probably not be met in the majority of cases. It is especially frequent—and properly so—for the historian to become intrigued by the new world of data processing and to press on past his original objectives to ask new kinds of questions of his data. All of this means that the programmer's services may be required for more than a fortnight.

A third alternative in the programming dilemma strikes middle ground between learning to write one's own programs and hiring some indifferent graduate student. Most computing centers have *packages* of pre-written programs on file, duplicates of which are available to users. A packaged program is a set of cards in the center's "library" (often just recorded on a tape), designed to perform some specific task. One standard library subroutine produces cross-tabulations; others find measures of central tendency, such as the average or median; still others do more complex computations, such as correlations. To the deck of cards the center gives him, the user has only to supply the few instructions the operating system requires, tell the computer what format the data have (what fields are where on the cards), and specify the output desired (what labels should be printed out and such). Most common among these "canned" subroutines are the SSP programs, statistical routines built right into the bowels of the IBM 360s, and the "biomedical" (BMD) programs, which computing centers supply in card form.

At least three *systems* of packaged programs are currently available to social scientists, and most computer centers will have acquired one of them. First, there is the "Statistical Package for the Social Sciences" (SPSS), developed at the Stanford University Computer Center and distributed by the National Opinion Research Center in Chicago. A second is called OSIRIS (after the god), and comes from the Inter-University Consortium for Political Research at the University of Michigan. A third, shortly to be discussed in detail, is DATA-TEXT, the work of the Department of Social Relations of Harvard University.[6] The local computer center will have an index to the program packages and systems it can supply to the user.

All these systems of packaged programs have advantages and disadvantages. Some sets of packages, such as OSIRIS, are relatively "format-bound." That means they will only accept input data prepared in rigidly predetermined form, with each field a certain number of columns wide, or with a blank column between each field, or with the proviso that no blank fields or units with missing cards be used. Other packages, such as DATA-TEXT and SPSS, permit great flexibility in the form of the input data, but at the disadvantage of being "unit-bound." This means they will treat the unit in which the coding was done as the unit of analysis, refusing unless prompted

[6]Edmund D. Meyers, Jr., gives an overview of the packaged programs currently in use in "A Survey of Social Science Computing Systems," a pamphlet available from the Sociology Department of Dartmouth College. Douglas K. Stewart briefly reviews such canned programs as the BMD package in "Computer Packages for Social Analysis," *Historical Methods Newsletter*, 1:2 (March, 1968), 1–2. And Michael Margolis discusses OSIRIS and SPSS in detail in "New Computer Packages for the Analysis of Social Science Data," *Historical Methods Newsletter*, 3:2 (March, 1970), 15–18.

by devious tricks to either disaggregate the data to a lower level, or aggregate them to a higher one. In projects that use manuscript census data, for example, the coding will usually be done at the level of the household, because each separate entry in the census schedule represents a separate house on the block. Yet for purposes of analysis, the historian might prefer to take as his unit the individual within that household, or indeed to aggregate separate houses to the level of the neighborhood, and use that as his basic unit. Thus each set of packaged programs will have its own benefits and costs. With some, the benefits of being able to range over different levels of units outweigh the costs of unbending format impositions, of the need for possible recoding of data, and of special problems posed by missing data. With others, the great versatility of format and the system's willingness to accept incomplete data override the cost of being frozen into a given unit of analysis.

I would like to pay special attention to one set of packaged programs—DATA-TEXT—both because I am more familiar with it than with any other, and because most historians will find it on balance most suitable to their own requirements. DATA-TEXT is a self-contained system of programs designed partly for the numerical analysis of data, partly for the content analysis of text.[7] Unlike regular source programming languages like COBOL or FORTRAN, DATA-TEXT users have merely to keypunch on a few control cards instructions written in something like plain English. These instruction cards then activate subroutines in the DATA-TEXT system, which go on and

[7]Arthur S. Couch, *The DATA-TEXT System: A Computer Language for Social Science Research* (preliminary manual, June, 1969, available from Department of Social Relations, Harvard University). An introduction is Judith E. Selvidge and Theodore K. Rabb, "DATA-TEXT: A Simple and Flexible Programming System for Historians, Linguists, and Other Social Scientists," *Computer Studies in the Humanities and Verbal Behavior*, 1 (1968), 107–14. DATA-TEXT is ideal for one computer application to historical research entirely ignored in this book: textual analysis. Although most historians will use computers for data processing, some, such as Gilbert Shapiro (see above, p. 20), will have projects involving counting the frequency of phrases or key words in documents. This is the end to which computers serve scholars in languages and literature. Readers interested in pursuing this application further should consult the journals, *Computer Studies in the Humanities and Verbal Behavior* and *Computers and the Humanities*, almost every issue of which reports some new project or technique using textual analysis. See also the bibliography published by Paul Kleppner in the *Historical Methods Newsletter*, 2:4 (September, 1969), 17.

tell the machine to execute the job. These subroutines would have to be written from scratch by a programmer using FORTRAN or COBOL. They are already present on the DATA-TEXT tape, which computer centers buy and mount on their computers. DATA-TEXT's virtue as a set of canned programs is its flexibility, for it may double not just for one or two standard packaged programs, but for hundreds of different programs, which would handle a limitless variety of tasks. All the user has to do is type out on a keypunch machine a few control cards that sound very much like the normal research instructions—although a little more abrupt—a historian or a sociologist would give his assistant. The DATA-TEXT system takes over from there and tells the computer in machine language exactly what to do.

A brief description of how the DATA-TEXT system works will make its virtues clearer to the reader. First, the DATA-TEXT user writes a format statement, to tell the machine how many data fields he has and how wide each is. Second, he specifies through a series of control cards which variables he wishes to use in the analysis, and how they are to be scaled. Finally, he types out the computations the system is to perform upon these variables. If he wishes cross-tabulations, for example, the user merely punches on an IBM card the following: *COMPUTE CROSSTABS (2,3,4 BY 1). The computer will thereupon produce three tables, variable 1 along the vertical axis of each, variables 2, 3, and 4 along the horizontal axes. If the reader wishes to see the frequency with which each code in a certain field appears, he writes on a control card: *COMPUTE FREQUENCIES (1–4). Thereupon the machine prints out the number of times each code in fields 1 to 4 is used. The simple instruction to compute frequencies without any subsequent parenthetical designation will produce the frequency distribution of every variable in the data file.

Although the reader will be able to appreciate the significance of some of DATA-TEXT's statistical options only after reading my chapters on statistics, I want to mention a few of the system's more elaborate capabilities here. The admonition to *COMPUTE STATISTICS without further ado brings from the computer the number of cases in each field, their average value, their variance, standard deviation, and skewness—measures of how values are concentrated or dispersed around a central point. The card *COMPUTE CORRELATIONS produces correlation coefficients, and if desired the level of significance of each, for all possible combinations of items of information. DATA-TEXT calculates all the standard nonparametric statistics: chi-square, gamma, and so forth, in a similar manner. The names of all these statistics may be meaningless to the reader at this juncture. The point is the effortless simplicity the system brings to computer programming.

DATA-TEXT handles with ease problems of incomplete data. Some cards may be missing from some units, or many fields may be blank: the system is indifferent. It accepts the most miserable data with aplomb. If the historian wants to combine fields, create new variables from combinations of old ones, have the computer recode data cards and punch them out, select only certain units for processing while omitting others, include units only if a given variable has a certain value, DATA-TEXT can do it. If the historian wants his tables clearly labeled, with neat, readable designations of what each field and row, each separate table and subtable represent, DATA-TEXT can do it.

The user of the DATA-TEXT system need bear only two things in mind. First, each unit in the deck must have an identification number no more than six columns long. Second, the system is highly unit-bound. The unit of analysis must be absolutely clear, whether counties, individuals, households, ships, charters, or whatnot. Changing units of analysis—as for example going from the level of the individual to the level of the household in analyzing census returns—is difficult though not impossible. Combining units together to form new units is also a chancy procedure, for the system will not budge if it cannot rigorously classify all input into separate units. Readers should also note that DATA-TEXT is cumbersome in analyzing published aggregated census data, for the system treats the census district, and not the people being enumerated, as the unit of analysis.

The manual for the system contains a clear, extensive introduction for laymen. A historian should be able to sit down with it and in several hours' time begin writing his own control cards. He is able to dispense entirely with the assistance of a programmer, presented by the system with tools for almost every conceivable analytic possibility.

If I have made DATA-TEXT sound like a combination of the Seabees and Superman, it is partly from nostalgia, for DATA-TEXT is a dying system. The system was designed to work only on the IBM 7094. And now that computer is everywhere being replaced by the IBM 360s, which will not accept DATA-TEXT. At this writing, only a few major computer installations retain their 94s and in most places the shift to the 360 has forced abandonment of DATA-TEXT, a comment on the pace of technological change in the area of computer research.[8] In the near future, however, the system should become available again. Some of DATA-TEXT's original inventors, members of Harvard's Social Relations Department, are now rewriting it for the IBM 360. If DATA-TEXT does reappear, readers will be able to ignore most of what I have said about the programming dilemma, and rely instead upon the system's handful of control cards to instruct the computer.

Figure 4–3 sums up the essential steps in processing quantitative data. In the first three chapters of this book we discussed these procedures in detail, starting first with the design of the codebook, then moving to technical information about coding, keypunching, and card handling. We have concluded this section by examining the programming dilemma: How is the historian, who conceives of the computer as a kind of Rube Goldberg contraption, to communicate with it? Let me reiterate one point. With every step in data processing there goes a corresponding checking stage. The original codebook is checked and tested against a sampling of data before the serious coding begins; the accuracy and consistency of the coding are checked through a subsequent recoding and comparison, an indispensable process when dealing with nonstandardized, qualitative source data; the keypunching is checked by putting a sampling of the finished cards through a card verifier. And, though I have not

[8]Another comment on this rapidity is the experience of H. J. Dyos' team of researchers, who worked with nineteenth-century English census data. For several years their data processing went slowly, as they tried to rewrite existing packaged programs to suit their needs with less than satisfactory results. Then, reports Dr. Dyos, DATA-TEXT came along, the use of which could have spared them this agony in the first place. By 1969, however, a year after the publication of the Dyos article, DATA-TEXT itself had vanished almost everywhere. See "The Possibilities of Computerising Census Data," in H. J. Dyos, ed., *The Study of Urban History* (London: Edward Arnold Publishers Ltd., 1968), p. 94.

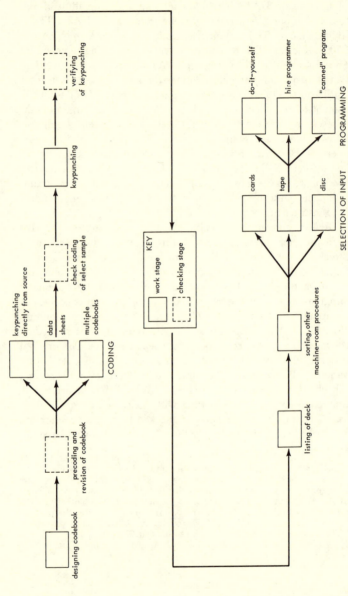

Figure 4—3 Processing the data: a model.

designing codebook → precoding and revision of codebook → keypunching directly from source / data sheets / multiple codebooks

CODING

keypunching → check coding of select sample → verifying of keypunching

KEY
work stage
checking stage

listing of deck → sorting, other machine-room procedures → cards / tape / disc

SELECTION OF INPUT

do-it-yourself / hire programmer / "canned" programs

PROGRAMMING

indicated so on this chart, even the programming should be checked by taking some machine-produced result—one of the columns in a cross-tabulation, for instance—and comparing it to a figure computed independently from the original source. Only if both totals jibe can the historian confidently put the sheets of computer results between the black covers of special output binders, and begin the analysis.[9]

[9]Increasingly common among historians is the *secondary* analysis of someone else's machine-readable data. A warning, therefore, is in order about the mechanics of trading information. If the historian gives the computer tape with his data to another scholar, or gets from elsewhere a tape with data he wishes to analyze, he must be sure to know the answers to the following questions (the questions may not make sense to him, but the answers will be vital to the programmers and computer operators who work with the tape):

What is the record length?
What is the record form?
What is the blocking factor?
What is the density of the tape?
How many tracks does the tape have?
Is the tape labeled, and if so, how?

5

Analyzing
the Results:
Descriptive Statistics

The mechanical part of this guide is now finished. Readers who know exactly what they want the computer to do for them, who can envisage in their mind's eye precisely how they wish the results to appear, may stop reading. I suspect that at this point relatively few books will in fact snap shut, for many historians may appreciate some advice on the *interpretation* of quantitative material as well as on its preparation and processing. As a rule, historians are unfamiliar with statistics and with procedures of quantitative analysis in general.[1] A book on computer applications to historical research would therefore do its readers a disservice if it left them in the dark on how to fully exploit the computer's capacities for analyzing (not just for manipulating) data, or if it failed to mention some simple statistical ways of getting the most out of quantitative evidence. The last part of this book accordingly takes up a few important points about statistics for historical research.

[1]Charles Tilly has recently pointed out the reluctance of French scholars to go beyond the simplest kinds of data analysis. ("Quantification in History, as seen from France," forthcoming in a special issue of *Explorations in Entrepreneurial History*.) Aside from American economic history, where quite sophisticated interpretations of quantitative data are now being done, I know of no area of history not embarrassingly behind the most elementary freshman social science course in data analysis.

Statistical techniques are useful in answering two kinds of questions historians frequently ask: the who, what, when, where, and how questions of describing events, and the why questions of analyzing them. In this chapter we shall see how data may be simply and clearly presented for descriptive purposes; in the following one we shall review some of the common statistical ways of finding associations and relationships between events.[2]

FREQUENCY DISTRIBUTIONS

The first kind of output the historian should get from the computer is a *frequency distribution*; that is, simply, he will have the machine tell him how often each code in each field was used, how his cases are distributed. A frequency distribution of variable 69 (most recent occupation) in the hypothetical study of the Paris June Days (see Appendix) might appear as in Table 5–1. The computer would print out all the occupational codes used (designated in the output as "values"), the number of times each occurred in the data deck, and the percentage of the total each occupation represented. Having finished variable 69, the machine would go on to variable 70 (first socio-professional status), and so on through all the variables in the codebook. DATA-TEXT produces such frequency distributions at the behest of a single control card. Standard packaged programs, many already built into the system, for this are available at computer centers. Social scientists once had to labor for hours over card sorters in order to produce the kind of information that now can be neatly tabulated by computers.

[2]Historians working with social and political data will find V. O. Key, Jr., *A Primer of Statistics for Political Scientists* (New York: Thomas Y. Crowell Company, 1954; paperback edition) the best introduction to elementary statistical analysis. Those working in economic history will prefer Samuel Hays, *An Outline of Statistics*, 7th ed. (London: Longmans, Green & Co. Ltd., 1966). Two other brief basic texts are Abraham N. Franzblau, *A Primer of Statistics for Non-Statisticians* (New York: Harcourt, Brace & World, Inc., 1958), and P. G. Moore, *Principles of Statistical Techniques: A First Course, from the Beginnings* (Cambridge: Cambridge University Press, 1964). None of these works requires any more knowledge of mathematics than most historians are likely to possess. Those who wish to freshen up their knowledge of mathematics, however, in preparation for more advanced statistical operations, are referred to Helen M. Walker's classic text: *Mathematics Essential for Elementary Statistics*, rev. ed. (New York: Holt, Rinehart & Winston, Inc., 1951).

Table 5–1. Sample Frequency Distribution: Example Taken from Codebook of June Days Arrests

	value*	number†	per cent‡
variable 69: most recent occupation ($n^§$ = 5000)			
agriculture	10	83	1.7
agricultural laborer	11	412	8.2
agricultural smallholder	12	188	3.8
forests	13	56	1.1
fishing	14	20	0.4
• • •			
variable 70: first socio-professional status ($n^§$ = 5000)			
unskilled	1	1000	20
semiskilled	2	3000	60
skilled	3	500	10
other	4	500	10

*value = actual code used to designate occupation, status, and so on
†number = number of times the code appears in the field
‡per cent = per cent each code in the field represents of the total number of cases in the field
§n = number of cases for which information exists

Calculating ("getting out," as computer people say) the frequencies is the first step in analyzing the results, for two reasons. One is that frequencies are needed in order to write the so-called final codebook. The researcher should go back to his tattered codebook one last time and in the margin enter the number of times each code in each field was actually used. This will permit him to disregard unused codes in the subsequent analysis, to see which fields have not worked out, to identify the variables that should be combined, the codes that may obviously be collapsed, and in general to assay the distribution of his data. The final codebook will also be useful in identifying "illegal codes," which is to say coding mistakes. If the values in field 46 (department of birth) may never be higher than 94, the presence of 96s and 97s in the frequency distribution will indicate the need for some checking. One might, for example, refine the final codebook by producing separate frequency distributions for each decade, and then indicate in the margin the number of times the various codes appeared in different periods, along with a grand total. This will permit the researcher to spot changes over time, or over place, or whatever, at the outset.

analyzing the results: descriptive statistics

A second reason for calculating frequency distributions at the very beginning is to give the researcher a sense of his data. The percentage figures help him look over the values in each variable, so that he begins to feel his way into the material. Acquiring such a sense of the distributions is an absolute precondition to proceeding with higher levels of analysis, where the complexities and anomalies so carefully provided for in the codebook will be effaced by the generality inherent in statistics.

CROSS-TABULATIONS

After calculating the frequency distributions, the historian will move to a second device for spreading the data out in front of him, the cross-tabulation (known to initiates as a "cross-tab"). A cross-tabulation is merely a table that classifies one variable in terms of another variable. A table is a statistical device so elementary that even historians are comfortable with it. Almost all of them use simple tables, or at least think in terms of them. Let me illustrate exactly how a cross-tabulation works with the idea of the chronological table. Table 5–2 is a familiar kind.

Table 5–2.   Yearly Number of Bankruptcies in Montreal, 1879–1885

1879	5
1880	20
1881	40
1882	55
1883	40
1884	35
1885	5
Total	200

Now, suppose Table 5–2 had two columns instead of one, representing the number of bankrupt individuals who were either Protestants or Catholics. The resulting table is shown in Table 5–3.

All we have done is to distinguish between kinds of bankruptcies, whether Protestant or Catholic, and to distribute the frequency of both over time. We have cross-tabulated one variable (year) by another variable (religion), using bankrupt individuals as the unit

Table 5–3. Yearly Number of Bankruptcies in Montreal by Religion

year	protestants	catholics
1879	5	0
1880	10	10
1881	15	25
1882	25	30
1883	15	25
1884	10	25
1885	0	5
Total	80	120

of analysis. All this is so painfully clear, except perhaps for the terminology, that I fear insulting the reader. Yet the next step in the
explanation is precisely where historians usually throw up their
hands in despair when confronted with it in the writings of a sociologist or economist.

Along with the variables year and religion, the student of Montreal also knew the age of the bankrupt individual. Just as he could
cross-classify year and religion in a perfectly comprehensible way, so
can he cross-tabulate the age and the religion of the bankrupt individuals. We get Table 5–4.

Table 5–4 Total Bankruptcies in Montreal by Age and Religion

	protestants	catholics
Young	20	30
Old	60	90

Is this not perfectly straightforward? The young bankrupts were
split two to three among Protestants and Catholics, the old in the
same proportion. Table 5–4 has in it the basic components of a
cross-tabulation: crossing two variables, each with two categories
in it, creates four little bins. The computer dumps the data into the
bins depending on whether the cards it examines show the individuals to be young or old, Protestant or Catholic.

But such a table can be easier to read and interpret if we pretty
it up a bit by drawing in some lines, and by adding totals to the
columns and the rows so that we will know altogether how many of

analyzing the results: descriptive statistics

each variable we have. Table 5–5 shows the expanded cross-tabulation.

Table 5–5. Sample Cross-tabulation by Age and Religion

	protestants	catholics	total
Young	20	30	50
Old	60	90	150
Total	80	120	200

The cross-tabulation in this table may stand as it is, having fulfilled its informative purpose. We know how the cases are distributed by religion and by age, and how many of each fall within the group of the other. Analytically, we may do nothing further with these specific data because the historian would not expect a businessman's religion to have much to do with his age at bankruptcy, and vice versa. Religion and age are both items of information in the data file, but they are not necessarily interrelated.

Cross-tabulations may have one other feature, percentages, which are useful if the researcher suspects that the two variables he is cross-tabulating might interrelate. Let us set up a situation in which we can say one variable helps "cause" another variable. The bankruptcy source reveals, alongside the man's religion, whether he had a long history of indebtedness before his bankruptcy. Treating religion as the independent variable (that is, as the causative factor) and debt as the dependent one (that is, the one being acted upon or produced), let us see how the tabulation looks that cross-classifies one against the other (Table 5–6).

Table 5–6. Sample Cross-tabulation of Montreal Bankruptcies: Religion by History of Indebtedness

	protestants	catholics	total
No previous debt	58	23	81
Previous debt	22	97	119
Total	80	120	200

Yet even if the historian suspects the presence of a relationship between the two variables, he will find it difficult to make much out

of the cross-tabulation in its present form: there are too many numbers to interpret clearly, and because they are absolute numbers
they do not reveal relative relationships. One can transform this
figure from a jumble of numbers to a simple interpretive instrument
by calculating the percentages of the column totals the figures in
each column represent (the two columns of cells and the outside
right column of totals). Witness the revised tabulation (Table 5–7).

**Table 5–7. Sample Cross-tabulation of Montreal Bankruptcies
with Percentages Added**

	protestants	catholics	total
No previous debt	58	23	81
	(72%)	(19%)	(40%)
Previous debt	22	97	119
	(28%)	(81%)	(60%)
Total	80 (100%)	120 (100%)	200 (100%)

In this table we look first at the distribution of the dependent
variable (indebtedness) and then ask how the independent variable
affected this distribution. The outside right column gives us the distribution of history of indebtedness independent of religion. We
then look to the cells running vertically to see how the factor of religion caused this distribution to change. Such a tabulation is read like
this: Whereas only 40 per cent of all bankrupt persons had no histories of indebtedness, 72 per cent of the Protestants were debt-free
(and a mere 19 per cent of the Catholics, half as few as among the
entire group). Or alternatively: Whereas 60 per cent of all bankrupts
had debt histories, 81 per cent of all Catholic bankrupts were previously indebted. In other words, Catholic bankrupts are about three
times more likely to have had previous debt than are Protestant
bankrupts. One may make of such results what one will. Would Max
Weber cheer, or roll in his grave, at such empirical derring-do?

Such are the purposes that cross-tabulations may serve. This particular operation is called percentaging the bivariate table (two variables, one horizontally, one vertically). The reader should note that
customarily the independent variable is the horizontal one, so that
to interpret the table one percentages *down* and compares *across*.[3]

[3]For a clear discussion of this device see Theodore R. Anderson and Morris
Zelditch, Jr., *A Basic Course in Statistics with Sociological Applications*, 2nd
ed. (New York: Holt, Rinehart & Winston, Inc., 1968), pp. 104–106.

Percentaging cross-tabulations is actually an analytic, not a descriptive technique, insofar as the two may ever be clearly separated, and the discussion of it logically belongs in the following chapter. Nevertheless it fits better here, because the historian will want to make cross-tabulations the central device for getting results from the machine. They permit him to see subgroupings and orders of magnitude in his data, as well as to find relationships among the items of information he has computerized. Cross-tabulations, with or without percentages, are the most dependable workhorses in all the social sciences for both presenting data and analyzing relationships.

The computer is useful in quantitative research precisely because it can print out with a simple instruction large numbers of tables like this, with all the percentages entered in and the numbers neatly arrayed. If the historian so wishes, he can ask his programmer (or use a canned program like DATA-TEXT) to run cross-tabulations of every variable in his file by every other variable. The tables are limited in width to the size of the computer paper, but can be any length the historian desires, their rows stretching down for page after page.

I would like to draw again upon one of my own projects for an example of the computer's versatility in producing cross-tabulations. The study of French strikes frequently requires the researcher to plot some variables by both department and industry. France has 11 basic industrial sectors, 90 departments. Much of my programming has been concerned with the production of great tabulations, 11 columns wide by 90 rows long, each table covering eight sheets of computer paper. A part of one such table is reproduced in Figure 5–1. (Note that the unit of analysis in this case is the number of strikers.) Each little box in this large matrix contains four pieces of information: the number of strikers, the percentage the strikers in this particular local industry represent of all the strikers in that department (the row percentage), the percentage these strikers are of all the strikers in that industry (the column percentage), and the number of strikers per 100,000 workers within that industry in that department (a striker rate). If the historian runs his eye along the marginal column figures, he sees the total number of strikers in each department, and how each department ranks, in percentage terms, in France as a whole. If the researcher runs his eye along the marginal row figures on the bottom of the last page, he notes how many

STRIKER RATES, INDUSTRY X DEPARTMENT
(NUMBER OF STRIKERS PER 100,000 WORKERS)
STATISTIQUE DES GREVES, 1890-1914

JANUARY 21, 1970

Each cell contains four stacked values: RATE* / NUMBER* / n.0(R) / n.0(C)

	AGRICULT	MINES	ALIMENT	CHEMICS	POLYGRPH	CUIRS	TEXTILES	METALS	TRAV METS	CONSTRUC	TRANSPTS	TOTAL	PRCT
AIN	0.* 0* 0.0(R) 0.0(C)	4032.* 864* 9.0(R) 0.0(C)	0.* 0* 0.0(R) 0.0(C)	4288.* 204* 2.0(R) 0.0(C)	211.* 22* 0.0(R) 0.0(C)	485.* 192* 2.0(R) 0.0(C)	552.* 2487* 25.0(R) 0.0(C)	0.* 0* 0.0(R) 0.0(C)	225.* 186* 2.0(R) 0.0(C)	1733.* 600(R) 60.0(R) 0.0(C)	12.* 104* 1.0(R) 0.0(C)	197. 10135	0.3
AISNE	26.* 613* 2.0(R) 0.0(C)	636.* 22* 0.0(R) 0.0(C)	194.* 431* 1.0(R) 0.0(C)	861.* 316* 1.0(R) 0.0(C)	562.* 115* 0.0(R) 0.0(C)	230.* 169* 1.0(R) 0.0(C)	2154.* 22537* 69.0(R) 3.0(C)	0.* 0* 0.0(R) 0.0(C)	673.* 1937* 6.0(R) 1.0(C)	780.* 4911* 15.0(R) 2.0(C)	96.* 1627* 2.0(R) 0.0(C)	510. 32678	0.9
ALLIER	21.* 592* 3.0(R) 1.0(C)	5347.* 7377* 4.0(R) 1.0(C)	548.* 505* 2.0(R) 0.0(C)	0.* 0* 0.0(R) 0.0(C)	4547.* 607* 3.0(R) 1.0(C)	146.* 55* 0.0(R) 0.0(C)	208.* 557* 2.0(R) 0.0(C)	5478.* 53565* 23.0(R) 6.0(C)	628.* 886* 3.0(R) 1.0(C)	1184.* 2081* 28.0(R) 1.0(C)	22.* 222* 1.0(R) 0.0(C)	471. 22983	0.6
ALP BS	2.* 20* 1.0(R) 0.0(C)	10882.* 811* 53.0(R) 6.0(C)	26.* 7* 0.0(R) 0.0(C)	2123.* 9* 0.0(R) 0.0(C)	0.* 0* 0.0(R) 0.0(C)	0.* 0* 0.0(R) 0.0(C)	97.* 53* 3.0(R) 0.0(C)	0.* 0* 0.0(R) 0.0(C)	0.* 0* 0.0(R) 0.0(C)	949.* 635* 42.0(R) 0.0(C)	22.* 222* 1.0(R) 0.0(C)	113. 1526	0.0
ALP HT	7.* 60* 3.0(R) 1.0(C)	584.* 15* 1.0(R) 0.0(C)	112.* 22* 1.0(R) 0.0(C)	0.* 0* 0.0(R) 0.0(C)	0.* 0* 0.0(R) 0.0(C)	0.* 0* 0.0(R) 0.0(C)	765.* 457* 25.0(R) 0.0(C)	148667.* 446* 25.0(R) 0.0(C)	197.* 29* 2.0(R) 0.0(C)	1805.* 776* 43.0(R) 0.0(C)	0.* 0* 0.0(R) 0.0(C)	136. 1814	0.0
SN-LOI	0.* 0* 0.0(R) 0.0(C)	12770.* 36973* 52.0(R) 6.0(C)	112.* 22* 1.0(R) 0.0(C)	249.* 17* 0.0(R) 0.0(C)	56?.* 108* 1.0(R) 0.0(C)	17.* 9* 0.0(R) 0.0(C)	467.* 244* 0.0(R) 0.0(C)	256361.* 21160* 30.0(R) 24.0(C)	886.* 8943* 13.0(R) 0.0(C)	1602.* 776* 43.0(R) 0.0(C)	5.* 7?* 0.0(R) 0.0(C)	920. 71470	1.9
SARTHE	7.* 60* 1.0(R) 0.0(C)	584.* 15* 1.0(R) 0.0(C)	0.* 0* 0.0(R) 0.0(C)	16421.* 1739* 28.0(R) 2.0(C)	1464.* 398* 6.0(R) 1.0(C)	22.* 215* 3.0(R) 0.0(C)	12.* 50* 1.0(R) 0.0(C)	180.* 446* ? ?	447.* 315* 10.0(R) 1.0(C)	864.* 32* 51.0(R) 0.0(C)	2.* 32* 1.0(R) 0.0(C)	104. 6153	0.2
SAVOIE	0.* 0* 0.0(R) 0.0(C)	1100.* 220* 2.0(R) 0.0(C)	42.* 23* 1.0(R) 0.0(C)	4966.* 521* 5.0(R) 0.0(C)	2787.* 383* 4.0(R) 1.0(C)	314.* 116* 1.0(R) 0.0(C)	882.* 1395* 14.0(R) 4.0(C)	25444.* 3180* 31.0(R) 4.0(C)	297.* 116* 1.0(R) 0.0(C)	3014.* 4256* 41.0(R) 1.0(C)	11.* 73* 1.0(R) 0.0(C)	304. 10283	0.3
SAVO HT	0.* 0* 0.0(R) 0.0(C)	11300.* 1175* 15.0(R) 1.0(C)	162.* 100* 1.0(R) 0.0(C)	7906.* 433* 4.0(R) 0.0(C)	330.* 25* 0.0(R) 0.0(C)	0.* 0* 0.0(R) 0.0(C)	517.* 775* 7.0(R) 0.0(C)	0.* 0* 0.0(R) 0.0(C)	3313.* 4061* 35.0(R) 0.0(C)	2375.* 3953* 34.0(R) 0.0(C)	114.* 602* 5.0(R) 0.0(C)	361. 11707	0.3
SEINE	381.* 2614* 0.0(R) 0.0(C)	5152.* 13665* ? ?	1133.* 12892* 2.0(R) ?	3160.* 1987* 3.0(R) ?	1208.* 19701* 28.0(R) ?	1573.* 14920* 3.0(R) ?		2717.* ?	2479.* 6576* ?	6576.* 330482* 52.0(R) ?	400.* 115056* 18.0(R) ?	1219. 638910	16.9

Annotation callouts on the figure: ① ② ③ ④ point to the AIN CONSTRUC/TRANSPTS boxed cell (1733 / 600(R) / ...); ⑤ ⑥ ⑦ point to the boxed TOTAL/PRCT example cell (471 / 22983 / 0.6).

YONNE	5. 11149 31.0(R) 1.0(C)	24. 677 0.0(R) 0.0(C)	395. 972 1.0(R) 2.0(C)	1561. 231 0.0(R) 1.0(C)	1128. 11492 7.0(R) 0.0(C)	204. 14 0.0(R) 0.0(C)	26. 120 1.0(R) 0.0(C)	109. 108 3.0(R) 0.0(C)	298. 175 5.0(R) 0.0(C)	221. 208 6.0(R) 0.0(C)	597. 12 0.0(R) 0.0(C)	96. 3749 0.1
SEN-INF	6547. 5753 4.0(R) 5.0(C)	537. 292 0.0(R) 0.0(C)	121. 163 0.0(R) 0.0(C)	1386. 29425 21.0(R) 4.0(C)	4264. 1284 1.0(R) 1.0(C)	4259. 17750 13.0(R) 5.0(C)	2783. 23431 17.0(R) 3.0(C)	1431. 60308 43.0(R) 12.0(C)	1298. 140236 3.7
HELFUR	0. 0 0.0(R) 0.0(C)	0. 0 0.0(R) 0.0(C)	0. 0 0.0(R) 0.0(C)	0. 0 0.0(R) 0.0(C)	0. 0 0.0(R) 0.0(C)	0. 0 0.0(R) 0.0(C)	0. 0 0.0(R) 0.0(C)	0. 0 0.0(R) 0.0(C)	0. 0 0.0
T.TOT / TOTAL / PCRT	89. 187705 5.0	523. 55041 1.5	9443. 598353 15.9	5112. 105877 2.8	1548. 59585 1.6	1648. 129293 3.4	1425. 802114 21.3	4583. 88821 2.4	1886. 344080 9.1	353. 48010 12.9	1297. 3171954 1000

Information in cells is for each industry within each department.

1. The number of strikers per 100,000 workers in the Ain's construction industry, 1890-1914 average.
2. The absolute number of strikers in the Ain's construction industry, 1890-1914 total.
3. The percentage which construction strikers compose of all strikers in the Ain department (Row percentage).
4. The percentage which construction strikers in the Ain compose of all constructions strikers in France (Column percentage).

Information in the vertical margin summarizes data by department.

5. The number of strikers per 100,000 workers in the Allier department, 1890-1914 average.
6. The absolute number of strikers in the Allier department, 1890-1914 total.
7. The percentage which strikers in the Allier department represent of all the strikers in France.

Information in the horizontal margin summarizes data by industry:

8. The number of strikers per 100,000 workers in the construction industry, 1890-1914 average.
9. The absolute number of strikers in the construction industry, 1890-1914 total.
10. The percentage which construction strikers represent of all the strikers in France.

Totals for all France are in the lower right corner. (Note that the percentages in both horizontal and vertical margins total up to 100.0 per cent):

11. The number of strikers per 100,000 workers in all France, 1890-1914 average.
12. The absolute number of strikers in all France, 1890-1914 total.

Figure 5-1 Sample cross-tabulation of strikes in France by industry and department.

strikers each industry contributed on a nationwide basis, and what each industry's relative contribution to the national total was.

Thus at a glance the historian may see how French strikes were situated in a given year, or 5-year, or 20-year period. (The example at hand is for the average of 1890–1914.) By plunging into the cells of the matrix, he may determine exactly which departments had what kind of industrial strikes, and how the strikes of each industry were distributed among the departments. It is quite useful to know, for example, that strikers in metal production in the department of the Allier were 23 per cent of the total number in that department, yet only 6 per cent of all the metals strikers in France. Moreover, wherever he looks the historian will find the striker rate, which reveals how the *intensity* of industrial conflict varied from one industry to another within a given department, from one industry to another at the national level, and so on.[4]

MEASURES OF CENTRAL TENDENCY

After the historian has produced a number of cross-tabulations in his first few weeks of dealing with the computer, he will probably start to feel bloated. By now, seas of square little boxes rise up at him even in his dreams. Sooner or later, he will decide he has acquainted himself sufficiently with the fundamental proportions of the phenomenon, and wish to begin generalizing, drawing together. We have already seen how data that are interrelated as independent and dependent variables may be analyzed with cross-tabulation percentages. But we have yet to propose solutions for abstracting and aggregating data on variables that, at this point in the analysis at least, the historian wishes to treat purely descriptively. Here I want to suggest two devices for bringing together the information

[4]As useful as cross-tabulations are for the scholar's own purposes in studying his data, I believe they should be avoided as a means of communicating results in publications. Most readers of historical literature are unfamiliar with the device and will be put off by its appearance. There are also more efficient ways of conveying information to even a statistically sophisticated audience than tabulations packed full of data. Robert McKenzie and Allan Silver, for example, use bar graphs to illustrate cross-tabular information. See *Angels in Marble: Working Class Conservatives in Urban England* (Chicago: University of Chicago Press, 1968).

which frequency distributions and cross-tabulations have spread out: measures of central tendency such as the mean (average) and the median, and graphs.

The arithmetic mean is the most commonplace of the descriptive statistics. In answering "how much" questions we almost instinctively have recourse to some kind of average figure. How much did the average Mississippi farmhand earn during the Depression? An average of a dollar a day. How many children did the typical peasant woman bear in her lifetime? An average of 5.5. The mean, of course, is calculated by adding up all the values in a frequency distribution, and then dividing by the number of cases involved.

A signal disadvantage of the mean is its liability to distortion by extreme values. If most of one's cases cluster about some numerical midpoint, yet a few are extremely high or low, then the average will become misleading by giving undue (or insufficient) weight to those few extreme cases. Let us take as an example the historian working with income distributions. He will want to make statements about how the city's wealth is divided. If he adds all the incomes together, and then divides by the number of wage earners, the procedure for calculating the arithmetic mean, he will emerge with an unduly rosy picture of the city's prosperity. The relatively few high incomes count for so much more than the masses of low incomes that they pull the latter up statistically.

The median is preferable to the mean as a measure of central tendency when the cases are widely dispersed. The median number is simply that midway up the scale. If all the cases are lined up in a frequency distribution, one has only to start counting until the halfway point is reached. That is the median. In order to find the median, the student of urban prosperity would consult the frequency distribution of his income variable, divide the total number of cases by two in order to discover when to stop counting, and then just march along the list until he came to that midpoint. Its value would be the median figure. The median would give him a truer picture of incomes than the mean because it preserves the significance of the low incomes and resists the upward pull of the high ones.

The computer solves the computational difficulties the median presents to researchers with large data files. All that counting off and estimating of the median can become both laborious and inexact when there are a sizable number of cases. But the computer upon instruction can simply order the data in a distribution from high to low values, and bring forth the median figure.

The disadvantages of the median are precisely the advantages of the mean. For some purposes the historian will need a single figure that incorporates the real weights of each of his cases. Let us say that an urban historian is studying income distributions not in order to make statements about social class but to assay the fiscal health of the community. The middle classes pay more property tax than the lower ones, who may not pay any at all. So the historian needs a measure of central tendency that will weight the members of the middle classes more heavily than the lower. This, of course, is the mean. And the mean income in this city will be higher than the median because the median gives disproportionate effect to the smaller incomes. As a rule of thumb, one might say that if the historian fears the distorting influence of a few cases with high values, he should select the median; if he fears that a number of low values will be overconsidered (if, that is, he prefers the distribution to be weighted), he should use the mean.

The historian may feel at this point that he is caught between two fires in attempting to determine the central features of his data: on the one hand, the mean overemphasizes eccentric values; on the other, the median is biased in the direction of conformism. To get a sense of how reliable the median or mean are as descriptions of reality, the researcher should ascertain how the data are dispersed on the whole. If the values are grouped in a relatively tight manner about some central point, he can use such measures with confidence. If, however, they are spread out with considerable numbers of cases about the fringes and no tendency to pile up at the center, then the researcher will have to be wary of averages and medians. False friends, they announce a centrality that does not exist.

MEASURES OF DISPERSION

Fortunately, a few simple measures of dispersion may be brought to bear. One alternative is simply to state the range of values, along with mean or median. Thus, for example, in examining the cargoes of merchantmen that set out from Boston it is useful to know that the smallest cargo was worth $500, the greatest worth $10,000, and the average was $8,000. However, the presence of a few quite aberrant values may make the range meaningless, just as a single dwarf on the rolls of those eligible for induction into the French army would make the bottom of the height range three feet.

Statisticians work with a measure called the "average deviation." They calculate this by subtracting each value from the mean or median, adding up the absolute values of all these individual deviations, and then dividing the sum by the number of cases. The average deviation will thus indicate how much dispersion is found among the group of values.

Those scholars working with sample data will prefer to the average deviation another measure of dispersion named the "standard deviation." The logic involved here is that the diversity within a population as a whole might be much greater than that within the sample group. If the researcher wishes to generalize the findings of his sample data to the entire population, then he must try to make the extreme cases within the sample as deviant as possible from the central body of cases. Even if, for example, it is found that a sample group of eighteenth-century families had between two and four children apiece, one might not unreasonably think that the real range among the population as a whole would be zero at the bottom, and perhaps 15 or so at the top. To gain a rough notion of how great this dispersion among the real population might be, the deviations from the mean are first calculated, each of them is then *squared*, whereupon these squares are added up, the total is averaged, and the square root of that figure calculated. The squaring removes the high values much farther than the low values from the center, thus making it more likely that the sample data encompass the extremes found in the real population. This is the standard deviation, different from the average deviation only in that it involves squares and square roots. A moment of reflection upon his high school arithmetic will remind the reader what these creatures are. Should he wish to spare himself the trouble of calculating squares and square roots, he may find them for a wide range of numbers in any handbook of standard mathematical tables, and in the appendices of many statistical textbooks as well.

analyzing the results: descriptive statistics **95**

A final measure of dispersion, skewness, is slightly more high-powered than the first two mentioned. Skewness tells whether a large number of cases are bunched either above or below the midpoint of the distribution. A statistician would think of these things in graphic terms. The distribution of cases may be represented as a curve. The curve line of the graph will describe the shape of a bell if the distribution is even, with few cases at the extremes, and larger and larger numbers until a peak at the midpoint is reached. A second's pause will convince the reader that in a symmetric distribution the mean and the median are the same, which means they are at the same point on the graph. Asymmetry arises, however, when the curve is foreshortened because of a paucity of either high or low scores. Skewness is a measure of this asymmetry, or lopsidedness. Whereas the average deviation reveals the amount of variability within the distribution, it says nothing about symmetry and asymmetry. That is, it does not reveal whether most of the cases are above or below the mean.

An example will make clearer this talk of skewness and curves. An historian is studying the value of cargoes dispatched from eastern seaports. He finds most of the cargoes leaving Boston to be worth something in the neighborhood of $10,000, but also a very few worth only hundreds of dollars. On the other hand, he discovers most of the cargoes leaving New York to be about $4,000 in value, but a very few worth over $15,000. How are the data on cargoes in each of these two ports skewed?

One calculates skewness by subtracting the median from the mean value. (Some statisticians would substitute the "mode" for the median in this calculation. Yet the mode—the single most frequent value—will have relatively little application in historical writing, and therefore I have not discussed it here.) If the distribution of cargo values is skewed to the right, as in the case of New York with its few extremely valuable shipments alongside a mass of middling ones, the mean value will be higher than the median. This is a positive skew. If the distribution of cargo values is skewed to the left, as in the case of Boston with its few paltry shipments alongside a mass of precious ones, the mean value will be lower than the median. This is a negative skew.[5]

[5]Hubert Blalock's discussion of this is to be recommended: *Social Statistics* (New York: McGraw-Hill Book Company, 1960), pp. 57–60.

Historians have had little use for such measures of dispersion as skewness because they normally do not work with sample data, and in their customary "total universes" of data it has been patently clear whether the median was higher or lower than the mean. However as they turn to samples, wherein it is risky to intuit distributions, or as they apply computer techniques to large populations, wherein the distribution of some characteristics within a subpopulation may not be totally obvious, they will need to work with things like skewness.

GRAPHS

The next step in describing data brings us to graphs. We are now nearing the end of the discussion of descriptive statistical techniques, having first started with such devices for spreading the data out as frequency distributions and cross-tabulations, and then moving to measures of central tendency for concentrating and summarizing facts. The graphing of time-series data represents a combination of these two modes of analysis, for on the one hand a summary figure is required for each year, whereas on the other data are dis-aggregated by being distributed throughout a number of years.

Historians will be complimented to discover that social scientists often refer to graphs—the plain old garden variety, which show the percentage of Democratic vote increasing in the 1930s or the peasant standard of living falling in the 1780s—as "historigrams."[6] A corre-spondingly elaborate set of techniques exists for analyzing graphical data that run over time, a subject I shall not take up here because it goes beyond my modest purpose of instructing readers in the first preliminary steps of studying computer output. Instead I shall limit myself to a few obvious points about graphs.

The main purpose in using graphs is to make easily visible some historical trend. Since the objective of graphs is clarity, the graphs should be as easy to read as possible.

There are several precepts to follow in designing good graphs. One is the use of logarithmic scales. Here it is a question of the scales in the left-hand margin of the graph, showing the magnitude

[6]Hays, for example, distinguishes between a "histogram" and "historigram" in *Outline of Statistics*, pp. 38, 98; the former is the graphical representation of data with bars, the latter the graphing of time-series data in general.

of the phenomenon (the height of the graph line) each year. What is the researcher to do, for example, if one year's value is very much higher or lower than another year's? The cost of bread will be many times higher in Germany for the years 1921–1923 than for 1911–1913. A graph that represented bread prices from the 1890s to the 1930s in Germany would have to be constructed with a scale of gigantic range in order to encompass the different prices of that 40-year period, a scale with subdivisions so minute as to obscure potentially significant variations that occurred from one year to the next. The solution is to use logarithmic scales rather than absolute ones. The vertical axis of a logarithmic scale is drawn up on the basis of the logarithms of the absolute numbers, not on the numbers themselves. This means that the upper ranges of the scale will be somewhat collapsed, permitting us to plot great variations in magnitude on a single sheet of paper. The range from 1 to 10 is a "cycle," that from 10 to 90 another "cycle," and so forth. One may buy graph paper with logarithmic scales in one or more cycles printed on it at stationery stores. (Ask for *semi-log* paper, so that the horizontal axis of the graph, on which one wishes to indicate the years, will retain its normal dimensions.)

Another point to keep in mind when presenting graphical data is the use of *moving averages*. This is a technique that comes to us from the economists, who like to be able to look at a graph of, say, the cost of living index for each month in the year and discern general trends from it. They apply the technique to graphs whose lines are likely to appear very bumpy and irregular in their pure state, making the discovery of trends difficult. A monthly cost-of-living graph, for example, might appear a mass of minute little humps and squiggles, the general direction of which is most difficult to determine. So the question becomes, how may one smooth out all those little irregularities so as to make the broad trends easier to interpret? An economist would call this removing seasonal variation. This is a question, incidentally, that historians are not prone to ask, for they attach some importance to the little humps and bumps distinguishing one year or month from another. Whereas a social scientist would be inclined to dismiss these small irregularities as the product of random or nonrecurring forces, a historian would say that the identification and analysis of such forces was the very heart of his enterprise.

Nonetheless, for some purposes the removal of short-term variations in a graph line is desirable. By making slight adjustments to
each of the yearly or monthly figures we permit them to demonstrate
more easily general trends. Let us assume that we wish to filter out
adventitious variations from a time series of the number of craft
licenses granted yearly in a German city, assuming further that
temporary, nonrepetitive influences will be smoothed out over intervals of three years. The computational procedure is to first take a
simple three-year average of the number of craft licenses, enter that
figure for the third year in the three-year bloc. Then drop out the
first year, add in the figure for the fourth year, and calculate a new
three-year average, entering that mean figure for the fourth year,
and so on. After the adjusted figures for the fifth, sixth, seventh, and
successive years have been calculated, the historian may go back
and estimate the figures for the first two years.[7] He will have
smoothed out the Alpine appearance of the graph, while retaining
some notion of the absolute number of craft licenses issued each
year.

The alternative to moving averages is simply to collapse the data
into larger blocs of time. Thus many economic historians like to contrast the performance of each of a series of five- or ten-year averages
to one another.[8] Although this has the advantage of simplicity and of
identifying at once the salient differences between longer time periods, it forecloses the opportunity of studying yearly variations.

A final point is the ease of comparing one phenomenon to another
that graphs make possible. When we talk of graphing two different
time series on the same graph we have already entered the realm of
analysis, for the two could be just as easily described on two separate
sheets of paper. One plots them together in order to determine if
changes in one line bear any relationship to changes in another.

[7]The procedure for calculating moving averages is explained in, among other
places, *ibid.*, pp. 100–105.

[8]This is the procedure the authors of the massive history of the French econ-
omy have chosen. See T. J. Markovitch, *L'industrie française de 1789 à 1964*, 4
vols. [J. Marczewski, ed., *Histoire quantitative de l'économie française*, vols.
IV–VII], in *Cahiers de l'Institut de Sciences Économiques Appliquées*, Series
AF. There are almost no yearly time-series data in Simon Kuznets' famous
Modern Economic Growth: Rate, Structure, and Spread (New Haven: Yale
University Press, 1966), to take another example. The data are aggregated into
blocs of 5, 10, or 20 years at least.

Figure 5–2 graphs the varying fates of Protestant versus Catholic businessmen in Montreal, the example with which we began this chapter. The data are much more comprehensible when presented in this manner than when presented as mere columns of figures. The reader is reminded that an array of statistical techniques exists for analyzing the covariation among graph lines. These are described in any basic statistics text.

I wish again to emphasize the usefulness of the computer in calculating statistics of central tendency and of graphical covariation. As we have seen, none of them is intrinsically difficult to work with or conceptually forbidding. Nevertheless in application they may require tedious spells over a bulky frequency distribution at a desk calculator. And the labor is duplicated many times if the historian wishes to break his data down into "subuniverses," and calculate averages, medians, standard deviations, and such for each region, each county, each industry, each city that he is investigating. The

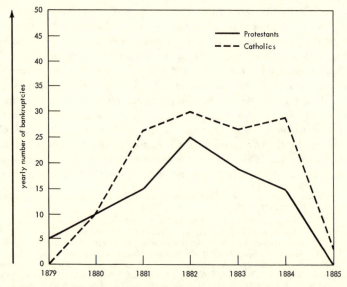

Figure 5–2   Sample graph: bankruptcy among Montreal businessmen, 1879–1884.

computer, with its prodigious capacities for storing and manipulating data, cuts right through this arduousness. Canned programs are available at every computer center for calculating these statistics, and as we have seen, such program packages as DATA-TEXT, OSIRIS, or SPSS produce them all automatically. The user has complete freedom to define the groups he wishes to work with and the subdivisions into which he wishes his evidence arranged. The computer guarantees him perfect accuracy. Researchers who anticipate making a lot of such statistical calculations might give some thought to using a computer, even if their data files are comparatively small.

THE RATE

One last descriptive statistic is the rate. The rate—an expression of a given quantity of something in terms of something else—is just as much an analytic as a descriptive statistic, for the historian uses it both to present data and to forestall a "why" question arising in his reader's mind. An historian of suicide might write that in a given year there were a large number of suicides in New York City and a small number in Keokuk, Iowa. The reader automatically thinks: "Ah yes, but is that because there are many more people in New York than in Keokuk?" Hence the student of suicides at the very outset prefers to present his data in terms of the total populations of the cities he is discussing. Rather than analyzing variations in the absolute number of suicides, he studies variations in their relative number, in suicides per 100,000 population. On a common sense level historians are thoroughly conversant with rates, and at once recognize the familiar percentage, which of course is just a rate of something per 100 of a larger something else.

A simple caveat regarding rates: The historian should make sure that the phenomenon under investigation, which constitutes the numerator of the rate, also is added to the larger population that serves as the rate's denominator. If the subpopulation in question is omitted from the larger population, the researcher will have not a rate but a ratio. As an example, one may take the study of illegitimacy. A simple kind of illegitimacy statistic is a rate of illegitimate children per 100 total births. The illegitimate births must appear in the denominator, if an illegitimacy rate is to be calculated. If the researcher compares illegitimate to legitimate births (illegitimate births/legitimate births) he will have a ratio; if he compares for a period of time illegitimate to total births (illegitimate births/total births) he will have a rate. The same relative relationship will prevail in a rate as in a ratio, but, in my opinion at least, a rate is much easier to read. The differences would be too elementary to mention, were they not occasionally forgotten or confused.

It is in the calculation of massive numbers of rates that the social, economic, or demographic historian may find the computer most useful. If I may again illustrate from the study of French strikes, one of the first analytic procedures Charles Tilly and I undertook was to examine the strikes of a commune, or department, or industry in terms of the total number of industrial workers employed in that unit. These strike rates are illustrated in Figure 5-1. The source material supplied only the absolute number of strikers, cross-classified by department and industry. Patterns of strike intensity could, however, only be discerned if we knew how large the total worker population was from which these strikers were drawn. So for each industry and each department in France, during each year between 1890 and 1935, we instructed the computer to produce rates of strikers per 100,000 people employed. Use of such rates immediately precludes the question, "But if Paris had more strikers, isn't that because Paris had more workers?"

Thus some historians may find the computer a godsend because of its ability to "mesh" files. Until this point, we have been thinking of data analysis in terms of a single input file alone. The historian would feed into the machine uniform data culled from his sources; the computer would dissect and analyze the internal dimensions of these data, and produce output. Yet in order to compute the rate of the phenomenon per 100 something else, an additional input file of external data is required. In order to compute rates of strikers per 100,000 industrial workers, the researcher must simultaneously give the computer the number of strikers in the industries and cities he is studying, and the numbers of industrial workers employed in them. In order to calculate suicide rates, the historian must have an input file of the absolute numbers of suicides, and a second file of the total populations of the census tracts, or cities, or whatever unit he is working with. The computer in its own storage area then meshes these two files and produces rates.

6

Analyzing
the Data:
Correlation

Having discussed how the historian may describe and cross-classify computer results, we now turn to how he may find statistical relationships among them. We have thus left the journalistic who, what, where, and how many questions to consider the why questions. It goes without saying that a clear line may never be drawn between description and analysis, the one being implicit in the other. I have employed this distinction partly for organizational convenience. Nevertheless the specific statistical techniques we now take up will be largely foreign to historians, who as a group have contented themselves with descriptive statistics, leaving the high-powered analytic ones to their colleagues in the "harder" social science departments. I am arguing that there is no reason why historians as well should not employ these devices if they feel their data are appropriate to them and their questions may be satisfactorily answered by them. After all, historians ask "why" questions of quantitative data all the time, doing so, however, with impressionistic techniques that may leave crucial relationships unexplored. In the next few pages we shall take up statistics that may bring out interesting associations. I emphasize that these pages are not to be thought of as an introductory statistical textbook: many good ones are already available, and space limitations command brevity. I introduce these statistics to give the reader an idea of some possibilities for inter-

preting his data. He will have to turn elsewhere for detailed guid-
ance.

TYPES OF DATA

Because different statistics are appropriate to different kinds of
data, we should first be clear about how a statistician might distinguish among the variables to be studied. In statistical terms, historians deal with three sorts of data: nominal, ordinal, and interval.

Nominal data refers to variables that are not quantitative, that
cannot be meaningfully added to or subtracted from one another.
In a codebook the fields for birthplace, or religion of mother, or
something similar would be nominal variables. It would make no
sense to subtract Sussex's code 02 from Yorkshire's code 14, or the
Democrat's code 2 from the Republican's 1. Nominal data, to elaborate the obvious, are not subject to quantitative analysis, yet may
be treated statistically nonetheless.

Ordinal data consist of variables whose scales have some quantitative relationship yet which are not entirely quantitative. A codebook field that called for the evaluation of an individual's wealth as
"great," "moderate," or "small" would contain ordinal data, for the
categories of the scale are ordered in a meaningful pattern from
high to low. The assessment of a district's political history as "tur-
bulent," "nominal," or "quiescent" would be ordinal because a statistical ranking is involved. Yet it is not a perfectly quantitative
ranking because the researcher would hesitate to attach much importance to say, an average of these values; nor are the numerical
distances between classes on the scale important.

Interval data are completely quantitative. They may be added and
subtracted, averaged, and otherwise manipulated. Their scales correspond to real numbers and not to artificial categories of measurement. The deputy's actual yearly income is interval data, as opposed
to such rough estimates of his wealth as "well-to-do" or "penurious,"
which is ordinal data. The county's actual population per square
mile is interval data, as opposed to the researcher's self-imposed
scale of densities, where $1 =$ very high density, $2 =$ high density,
$3 =$ moderate density.

analyzing the data: correlation

The majority of fields in historians' codebooks will concern either nominal or interval data, ordinal data being relatively unusual in quantitative historical research. In the 1940s, and 1950s, when social scientists had to process their data with card sorters rather than electronic computers, ordinal data enjoyed a burst of popularity. The researcher was forced to scale a complex multicolumn value into nine simple subdivisions that could fit into a single IBM card column, because the sorter could handle only single-column variables. Thus a man's age, which as interval data requires two columns, would be coded as one of the following ordinal categories: 1–9 years, 10–29 years, 20–29 years, etc. Fortunately, the computer put an end to the waste of data and the limitations of analysis that many ordinal variables represented. The intrinsic differences between the three kinds of data will be entirely clear to readers, who can see there is a difference between birthplace and income, just as there is a difference between desks and chairs. I mention this whole business only because some statistics are suited to nominal and ordinal data, some to interval.[1] In the ensuing discussion I will first explain statistics applicable to interval data, concentrating on the Pearson product-moment correlation coefficient. In a second section I will take up statistics designed for nominal and ordinal data, placing emphasis upon the chi-square test. The reader will be cheered to discover that the statistics themselves are not as off-putting as their names.

[1]Among excellent guides to these more advanced statistics are Theodore R. Anderson and Morris Zelditch, Jr., *A Basic Course in Statistics with Sociological Applications*, 2nd ed. (New York: Holt, Rinehart & Winston, Inc., 1968), and John H. Mueller *et al.*, *Statistical Reasoning in Sociology*, 2nd ed. (Boston: Houghton Mifflin Company, 1970), both to be recommended because they require little mathematical knowledge from the reader. Other useful textbooks in selecting the most appropriate statistic are Robert S. Weiss, *Statistics in Social Research: An Introduction* (New York: John Wiley & Sons, 1968), pp. 178–219; and Johan Galtung, *Theory and Methods of Social Research* (New York: Columbia University Press, 1967), pp. 204–39. An invaluable survey of already published research using various kinds of measurements is Charles M. Bonjean *et al.*, *Sociological Measurement: An Inventory of Scales and Indices* (San Francisco: Chandler, 1967); a systematic introduction to advanced statistics for those who care to learn their mathematical derivations, as well as learn the computational procedures, is Hubert M. Blalock, Jr., *Social Statistics* (New York: McGraw-Hill Book Company, 1960). An advanced guide to computerized manipulation of these statistics is Theodor D. Sterling and Seymour V. Pollack, *Introduction to Statistical Data Processing* (Englewood Cliffs, N.J.: Prentice-Hall, Inc., 1968).

analyzing the data: correlation

Historians are constantly asking questions that imply correlation. The most "conventional" diplomatic historians have probably mused that as international tension rises, the danger of war increases. Political historians of many countries have thought to identify a connection between the presence of rural smallholders and political conservatism. Certainly demographic historians have felt the need to test propositions like: there is a direct relationship between improvements in public health and increased longevity; or, as mothers abandoned breast-feeding, they had increasing numbers of children. Economic historians until recently have confidently asserted a relationship between railway construction and economic growth. And social historians have long been making statements about how the growth of cities brings about politically disoriented populations prone to experiment with violence and disorder. These kinds of questions about quantitative behavior are as old as the discipline. By linking pairs of variables in a causal, or at least an associational manner, they may be resolved statistically.

Here we take up the product-moment correlation coefficient, developed by the English statistician Karl Pearson. Although historians are familiar with the notion of correlation as a generic term for relationship, most will not recognize the term in its specific statistical sense. It has become in recent years the most common single statistic in social science research, and already in isolated instances of historical literature one notes its appearance. (The statistical symbol for it is r.)[2]

The principle of the coefficient of correlation is relatively straightforward. In order to understand it, we return to reconsider our by now familiar friend, the cross-tabulation. Figure 6–1 represents a simple cross-tabulation of two variables, the percentage of smallholders in a hypothetical country by district, and the percentage of conservative voters in each district of that country. Now, as we inspect this tabulation we note that the cells containing most of the districts are piled up along a line running from the lower left-hand

[2]The simplest discussion of correlation I have seen is V. O. Key, Jr., *A Primer of Statistics for Political Scientists* (New York: Thomas Y. Crowell Company, 1954), pp. 105–29; paperback edition.

analyzing the data: correlation

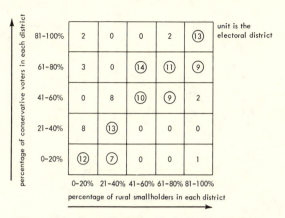

	0-20%	21-40%	41-60%	61-80%	81-100%	
81-100%	2	0	0	2	⑬	unit is the electoral district
61-80%	3	0	⑭	⑪	⑨	
41-60%	0	8	⑩	⑨	2	
21-40%	8	⑬	0	0	0	
0-20%	⑫	⑦	0	0	1	

percentage of conservative voters in each district

0-20% 21-40% 41-60% 61-80% 81-100%

percentage of rural smallholders in each district

Figure 6–1   Cross-tabulation illustrating correlation.

corner of the table to the upper right-hand corner. I have circled these boxes in pencil so as to make their concentration clear. This distinctive pattern indicates the presence of a positive correlation between the two variables: the higher the percentage of small-holders, the higher the percentage of conservative voters. If the pattern went the other way—with the fullest cells running along the *other* diagonal, from upper left to lower right—a clear negative correlation would be present. That pattern would translate into English thus: as the percentage of smallholders in a district increases, the percentage of conservative voters decreases. The reader will note that "negative" does not mean there is no correlation at all; there may be a close correlation, but the relationship between the variables is inverse: as one falls, the other rises.

If we take the lines out of Figure 6–1, and plot the actual districts in the form of dots, as in Figure 6–2, we get a graph called a "scat-tergram." Correlation is present when the dots appear to be closely grouped along a line running through the scattergram. The tighter the cluster, the greater the correlation. The slope of the line itself reveals whether the correlation is positive or negative. This line is called the "regression line" and may be plotted on the graph with the "least-squares" method. Although one may sit down and sketch in a rough regression line by rule of thumb, the least-squares

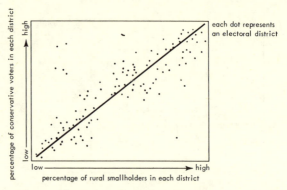

Figure 6–2 Sample scattergram.

method permits researchers to describe its position mathematically. I shall not go into what "least-squares" means here.[3] The point of all this is that the historian may graphically envisage the concept of correlation by thinking about the regression line and how it is drawn. Every pair of variables arrayed in a cross-tabulation will have a regression line, although if the correlation is not close, and the dots are merely dispersed across the page, the line will be meaningless.

A correlation coefficient is nothing more than a mathematical way of describing how well most of the dots on the scattergram hug the sloping regression line. A high correlation means the dots are tightly grouped along the line, a low one means the fit is poor. A statistician would see this matter of dots and lines differently. He would say the correlation permits us to say how much of the variation in one variable we can explain in terms of the variation in another. How well can the proportion of political conservatives be accounted for by the proportion of rural smallholders?

The correlation coefficient is easy to interpret because its upper limit is a $+1$, its lower limit a -1. If the relationship between smallholding and rural conservatism were perfect and positive, the correlation would be a $+1$ ($r = 1$); if it were perfect and negative, which is to say that conservatives were found everywhere smallholders

[3]See V. O. Key's excellent discussion, *ibid.*, pp. 73–100.

analyzing the data: correlation

were not, the correlation would be a −1 ($r = -1$). Of course in real life such perfect relationships simply do not occur. Too many additional variables intervene to make such absolute determinism possible, and extremely high correlations are those on the order of .8 or .9. The absence of correlation is indicated by a very low number, a .2 or a .1 or less.

One warning about interpreting the correlation coefficient: Because these statistics are based on squares and square roots, their meaningfulness does not go up and down in neat arithmetic order. A .7 is not just one unit less important than a .8, but considerably less important. A .8 is not just twice but several times as interesting as a .4. Keep in mind that *the square of the coefficient is the amount of variance that the correlation explains.* In other words, a correlation of .4 "explains" 16 per cent (not 40 per cent) of the variance in one phenomenon in terms of the other; a correlation of .7 "accounts for" 49 per cent (not 70 per cent) of the change in one variable as a function of another variable.

When the historian is working with sample data, he should be aware of the *significance* level of the correlation. "Significance" is another of those words with a common sense meaning and a quite precise statistical meaning that is close but not identical to the familiar version. If a scholar has a sampling of data—such as 1 family in every 10 from census returns or 1 of every 5 men arrested in some insurrection—he will ultimately wish to generalize from his sample to the entire population of those polled in the census or arrested in the revolt. Statistical tests, which I will not here describe, permit him to know how much confidence he may place in the wider applicability of any correlation derived from the sample. These tests let the researcher know for what level of significance his results are valid. Historians who use correlations upon some "total universe" of data (in other words, upon any group other than a sample) may ignore the notion of significance. The statistical significance of a particular statistic is in no event to be confused with its theoretical significance, that is, with the degree of the association it measures.[4]

Useful as the correlation coefficient is, the historian must bear several warnings in mind before applying it indiscriminately. First,

[4]On statistical significance see Galtung, *Theory and Methods of Social Research*, pp. 372–83.

correlation works best when large numbers of units are involved. If the cases to be studied are a mere handful, the coefficients will have to be quite high to merit attention. As the number of cases included rises into the dozens, the threshold of meaningfulness drops, and coefficients of .4 or .5 may be viewed as important. No exact statistical procedures exist for relating the number of cases studied to the importance of the correlation, and the researcher will have to trust his intuition about the solidity of his results.

Second, the user of the correlation should take a look at the scattergram before applying the correlation coefficient to a pair of variables. Correlation coefficients work only on linear relationships. (A relationship is linear when a change in the value of one variable produces in constant proportion a corresponding change in the value of the other, from bottom value to top.) Other statistics must be selected (namely, the correlation ratio) for the analysis of data related in a curvilinear manner (which means that above or below a certain value of one variable the relationship either stops or reverses its direction). A glance at the scattergram will reveal the nature of the relationship, for the long diagonal cluster strewn along the graph is at once recognizable. It is acceptable for the user to substitute a cross-tabulation, as in Figure 6–1, for a regular scattergram, although computer programs exist that make scattergrams readily available.

Third, the user should treat data files containing a number of extreme cases in a special way. A few very high values ("outliers") that deviate from the general trend will badly distort the statistical relationship, weakening and concealing associations. Paris, for example, is an extreme case in France, its population being much larger and behaving differently than any other department's. Accordingly, if one is trying to find correlations among various socioeconomic characteristics of the French population by department, the Paris figures will have to receive special treatment because they are often extreme and they weigh so heavily in the balance. When outliers are a problem, the correlation should be calculated twice: once with the extreme cases in the file, a second time with them removed. This procedure will tell us just how much difference the presence of Paris makes; at the same time it lets us be true to the original record. An alternate means of minimizing the effect of extreme cases is to perform some kind of "transformation" upon the data. This means replacing the original observations with, for example, their logarithms or their square roots, in order to shrink the distance between the outliers and the central body of values.

Finally, and most important of all, the historian should remember that correlations do not mean causes. They say only that associations, or relationships if one prefers, exist between two variables. They do not say that one variable causes another, that one variable is automatically independent, the other dependent upon it. A correlation between two characteristics of the same unit may merely mean that both vary in response to the action of some third, or fourth, or complex combination of variables as yet unidentified. A correlation over time between the snowfall in London and the snowfall in Moscow does not mean that the snow in London causes the snow in Moscow to fall.

Historians who use correlations in their research will have special reason to rejoice at the availablity of the computer. The computation of a correlation by desk calculator can be a wearisome affair, particularly if a large number of cases is involved. Astronomical numbers are produced in the course of the operation, and much squaring and square rooting needs to be done. An entire working day can be consumed by figuring out and checking a single correlation if the operator is inexperienced and the number of units exceeds 100. In addition, the production of scattergrams by hand, or even of cross-tabulations to serve the purpose of checking for linearity and looking at the slope of the regression line, may require a great deal of time and energy. The computer does all this so fast. Special programs produce scattergrams from the machine, and of course canned programs such as in the DATA-TEXT or OSIRIS systems can evoke limitless numbers of cross-tabulations with ease. The computer can print out large matrices of correlations that run every variable in the deck against every other variable if the user so wishes. The historian who thereupon gets his ideas by flitting his eye down the columns of coefficients hunting for high ones is committing a parody of the analytic method. The point is that the computer makes child's play of computational procedures which in pre-electronic days frightened all but the most resolute away.

Other statistics, more sophisticated than simple correlation, are available for handling interval data, but the reader is advised to ascend into this rarefied air with caution. Basic statistics courses commonly end with the simple correlation, leaving the others for advanced students. Nonetheless, I will briefly identify the super-statistics so the reader will at least be aware they exist, should he encounter uncommonly difficult analytical problems. They are commonly called multivariate statistics, as opposed to the bivariate kind such as correlation coefficients.

The super-statistics were developed because people elsewhere in the social sciences are suspicious, just as historians are, of mono-causal explanations. The simple correlation is in a way a frustrating, foolish device because it tells us only the importance of a single factor in accounting for some phenomenon. Intuition alone, however, postulates that in "explaining" an event or a kind of behavior numerous different factors must be simultaneously considered. There might be a relatively low correlation between the presence of industrial workers and leftist voting in a nation as a whole, for example. Yet when one considers the areas where the workers were concentrated in large industrial establishments rather than isolated in small scattered firms, or where working class political organizations existed to mobilize support rather than leaving the workers uninformed and apathetic, a strong association between the presence of industrial workers and leftist politics might be noted. In this example we have gone from the monocausal hypothesis that workers mean radicalism to a more sophisticated model stating that at least three variables produce leftist voting: presence of working classes, concentration of the work force in large industrial establishments, and existence of worker political organizations.

If we ran each of these three independent variables against the dependent variable of radical voting, we would discover only moderately interesting correlations, for it is the simultaneous presence of the three that combines to mobilize support for radical candidates. A statistical device is required that will observe the effect of each of the three upon voting while "controlling" at the same time for the other two. Statisticians conceive these problems in terms of measuring the impact of one variable upon something while holding the other variables "constant." The theory behind all this is formidable, and the reader need understand little beyond the fact that statistical routines are available for studying the interaction of several factors at once, and that the analysis must not necessarily stop at the level of pairs.

These problems are dealt with through the techniques of multiple regression and the analysis of variance. They permit the researcher to assign a precise value to each of several variables in assaying the total impact of all of them upon some dependent phenomenon. The correlational statistics are used exclusively on interval data; the analysis of variance procedures permit the researcher to mix together interval, ordinal, and nominal variables in building a model. Lest the reader feel antediluvian for having never even heard of these super-statistics, I hasten to point out that until now only a handful of social scientists have worked with them, with the vanguard of users in the highly mathematical branch of economics known as econometrics.[5]

Unlike the simple correlation, which researchers unlettered in formal statistical and mathematical training can employ using statistics "cookbooks," multiple correlation and the analysis of variance require a sophisticated grasp of how statistical explanation works. Unlike the simple correlation, whose range from zero to one makes it easy to interpret, the final product of the super-statistics can be evaluated only by researchers who understand their stucture. I do not wish to overemphasize the pitfalls, for, owing to the availability of canned computer programs that simplify computation, multivariate statistics are rapidly becoming popular in many disciplines.[6] Nevertheless the difference in difficulty between understanding such elementary aids as average deviation or simple correlation and the

[5]Stuart Blumin is one historian to have used the super-statistics; he employed the two-way analysis of variance in a study of social mobility in Philadelphia between 1820 and 1860. See "The Historical Study of Vertical Mobility," *Historical Methods Newsletter*, 1:4 (September, 1968), 1–13.

[6]For an example of the use of multiple regression in the analysis of historical data, see Karl O'Lessker, "Who Voted for Hitler? A New Look at the Class Basis of Naziism," *American Journal of Sociology*, 74 (1968–1969), 63–69. O'Lessker's experience with multiple regression shows the hazards a scholar incurs when he uses routines with which he is not totally familiar. See the comment by Allan Schnaiberg, "A Critique of Karl O'Lessker's 'Who Voted for Hitler?'" *ibid.*, pp. 732–35.

super-statistics is like the difference in difficulty between under-standing Will Rogers' and Hegel's philosophies of history.[7]

STATISTICS TO USE WITH NOMINAL AND ORDINAL DATA

Until now we have talked mainly in terms of analyzing interval data, that is, variables already in ordered form where the intervals between values are steady and the differences meaningful. Much historical data, however, will be in nominal or ordinal form. How is it to be analyzed statistically? Just as the geneticist might ask: do mothers with a particular eye coloring tend to produce daughters with the same eye color (both nominal kinds of data), so an historian might ask: did the sons of government bureaucrats tend to follow in the footsteps of their fathers? Both variables referred to in this question are nominal. Whether the fathers and the sons were civil servants or not is decided merely with a yes or no, not with any kind of numerical scale on which the gradations are ordered from low to high and on which the values themselves have an arithmetic importance.

Social scientists have at their disposal a whole range of statistics for studying ordinal and nominal data. In the following pages I will discuss at some length one that historians may find useful. Before becoming involved in a detailed explanation, the reader might appreciate a general overview of these various statistics. Table 6–1 shows which are applicable to each of the three basic forms of data.[8]

[7]I know of no guide to multivariate statistics that can be understood without some basic knowledge of mathematics. Two introductions to multivariate analysis, however, are V. O. Key's brief account of multiple and partial correlation on pp. 147–53 of *Primer of Statistics* and Anderson and Zelditch, *Basic Course in Statistics*, pp. 163–85. One standard account of multivariate statistics is Blalock, *Social Statistics*, pp. 326–91.

[8]Table adapted from Galtung, *Theory and Methods of Social Research*, pp. 208, 228. For examples of applications of these nonparametric statistics to historical research, see Duncan MacRae, Jr., *Parliament, Parties, and Society in France, 1946–1958* (New York: St. Martin's Press, Inc., 1967), which uses Yule's *Q* to find associations between roll call votes; and Patrick and Trevor Higonnet, "Class, Corruption, and Politics in the French Chamber of Deputies, 1846–1848," *French Historical Studies*, 5 (1967), 204–24, which uses chi-square to test for relationships between regional origin and political affiliation, among other things.

analyzing the data: correlation

Table 6-1. Some Common Statistics

interval scale	ordinal scale	nominal scale
Correlation coefficient	Kendall's tau	Chi-square
Multiple regression	Yule's Q	Goodman-Kruskal's
	Goodman-Kruskal's gamma	lambda and tau
	Spearman's rho	Phi coefficient
	Chi-square	

I will leave all of these save one in obscurity. The so-called non-parametric statistics, which most of the above are, represent a true jungle for the uninitiated, for a host of factors govern exactly which ones are suitable to which research problems: whether the data are samples or entire populations; whether the cross-tabulations have four cells or more; whether the variables are ordinal or nominal, to name some considerations. In the remainder of this chapter we shall concentrate upon a single member of this bizarre array: the chi-square test. How does it work?

Statistics that handle nominal data (for which chi-square is mainly used, although it may also be applied to ordinal data) operate on a different principle than those for interval data. In the latter case, the statistic merely has to show if a change in one variable on a graph produces a change in the other. If we can partly predict the value of the one on the basis of the other, then the variables are statistically related. We are already familiar with this concept. Non-numerical data, however (nominal and ordinal), by definition have no precise, ordered values, and so statistics that were developed to treat such quantitative values are inapplicable to more qualitative ones.

The principle of statistics for qualitative (nominal) data is to ask not how the variables in question fluctuate with each other's movements (as the correlation coefficient asks), but how the data at hand would look if there were no relationship between them at all. If the two variables were interrelated in no way whatsoever, how would the distribution of their cases be different from the present one? If a bourgeois' accession into the French nobility were entirely uninfluenced by his financial status, how many fewer wealthy middle-class families would have seen their scions ennobled? If the region a congressman comes from is irrelevant to his voting behavior, how many fewer votes would cotton-goods tariffs have received from border-state congressmen, how many more from western congressmen?

In order to deal with such nonquantitative nominal variables as whether the offspring of a bourgeois family were subsequently ennobled (yes or no, how many of each?), we use the nonparametric statistics.[9] In what is jargonishly described as the "null hypothesis," some of these statistics first estimate the values the variables would assume were they entirely uncorrelated, and then see how far their real values deviate from these assumed ones. The nonparametric statistic examines the content of each cell of the cross-tabulation, calculates the difference between the real figure and the figure that would have been there were the two variables independent of each other, squares this difference, and finally adds up the squares to arrive at the statistic.

This is the principle of the chi-square test, the most common of the nominal family statistics that test reality against the assumption of independence. The procedure for obtaining chi-square is to subtract the real from the expected value of each cell, square each of the differences, divide these by the expected values, and then add up all the quotients.[10] The end product of these manipulations is written something like this: "x^2 (the symbol for chi-square) $= 30.96$, significant at the .01 level with nine degrees of freedom." To nonstatistical readers such intelligence is likely to be gibberish.

To understand how to calculate and interpret chi-square results, keep in mind that the statistic is computed from a cross-tabulation. The more cells there are in the tabulation, the more likely it is that the result will be a large figure. We allow for this by taking into

[9]The word "parameter" means simply some numerical characteristic of a population. One often hears the terms "nonparametric" and "parametric" used in connection with statistics. "Nonparametric" is actually a misnomer for non-interval parametric statistics, such as chi-square (as Johan Galtung explains in *Theory and Methods of Social Research*, p. 341); a procedure such as a rank test is genuinely nonparametric. "Parametric" refers to such interval data statistics as simple correlation. V. O. Key takes an iconoclastic view of the expression "parametric," calling it a word that "judiciously used, creates an appearance of erudition." (*Primer of Statistics*, p. 157.)

[10]I have simplified the logic of the statistic somewhat in this summary. For a clear account of the actual computational procedure, see Blalock, *Social Statistics*, pp. 212–20.

analyzing the data: correlation

account the number of cells in the table in actually interpreting the statistic. The first thing to do is to figure out how many "degrees of freedom" are in the table. In order to calculate the number of degrees of freedom, one multiplies the number of rows in the table minus one row, times the number of columns minus one column.

Some of these points may be illustrated with the sample chi-square calculation, as in Table 6–2. We assume a hypothetical student of the nineteenth-century Prussian bureaucracy wishes to determine the degree of association between social class of origin and the branch of the civil service in which the bureaucrat found himself. The table that checks out this problem has three rows down and three columns across (a "three-by-three" table, as one says). This table thus has $(3-1) \times (3-1) = 4$ degrees of freedom.

Table 6–2. Cross-tabulation Illustrating Chi-square* for Hypothetical Study: Nineteenth-century Prussian Bureaucrats

branch of civil service in which man served	social class of origin of bureaucrat		
	upper	middle	lower	TOTAL
financial	75	60	5	140
administrative	50	30	20	100
judicial	25	10	10	45
Total	150	100	35	285

Chi-square: 22.61, with 4 degrees of freedom (significant at the .01 level)

How about significance levels? Significance addresses the problem of chance results in chi-square. The basic principle of the statistic requires one to bear in mind the possiblity that the relationship is spurious, produced by chance and not by any intrinsic interrelationship between the variables. If it is possible that chance alone would have produced a given result more than 5 per cent of the time, then that result is usually worthless. The level of significance thus means the risk, measured as a percentage, that no relationship among the variables exists at all. A chi-square statistic "beneath the .05 level" means that chance would probably have generated the result no more than 5 per cent of the time. The same goes for the expression the ".02" and ".01" levels. These levels permit the user to judge how much confidence he may place in a given result. Chi-square results beneath the .01 level may be thought of as very reliable.

In order to determine the meaning of a chi-square result the user must consult a statistical table entitled "distribution of chi-square values," or some such thing, to be found at the back of standard statistics textbooks. He runs his eye down the far left-hand column labelled *df* or "degree of freedom" until he comes to the number of degrees of freedom his cross-tabulation has. Then he runs his eye across the row until he is able to position his chi-square result between two of the values given in that row, indeed determine that his result is higher than any number in the row. This tells him for what significance level his chi-square calculation is valid. The higher the level, the more valid. The chi-square result of Table 6–2 was 22.61, and we discover this is significant beyond the .01 level by looking across the row associated with 4 degrees of freedom to see where this score falls. In this case, 22.61 is higher than the last number in the row (with 4 degrees of freedom one would have to have a chi-square above 13.28 for validity at the .01 level), so we know the association shown in Table 6–2 is fairly strong. There is not one chance in a hundred that this result could have been randomly obtained.

A few warnings about chi-square. The number of cases in each cell should not be smaller than five, for zero-cells and those with little in them distort the result. Accordingly, the user may wish to combine a few of the rows or columns in the table in order to achieve the desirable number of cases in each cell. The cell contents must always be absolute numbers, never rates. (A statistician would say they must always be "frequencies," never "measurements.")

I have discussed chi-square at length because it has been the most frequently used of the nonparametric statistics. Yet it is not wholly appropriate for historians who have large numbers of cases in their data files, because when many units are involved almost all chi-square results are likely to prove "significant." Nor may it be used to compare a number of different tables one to another because chi-square has no absolute upper and lower ranges (such as the corre-

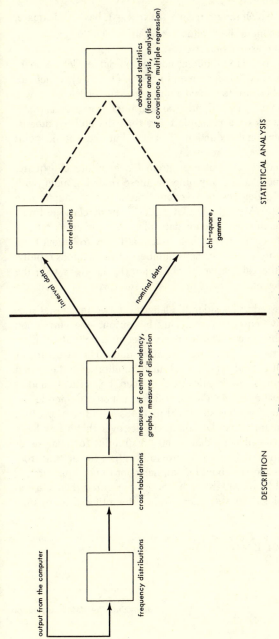

Figure 6—3 *Analyzing the data: a model.*

output from the computer

frequency distributions

cross-tabulations

measures of central tendency,
graphs, measures of dispersion

DESCRIPTION

interval data

nominal data

STATISTICAL ANALYSIS

correlations

chi-square,
gamma

advanced statistics
(factor analysis, analysis
of covariance, multiple regression)

lation coefficient, which ranges from a −1 to a +1, has). Chi-square, after all, measures more the likelihood that an association exists than the strength of the association itself.

For measuring association among nominal variables, let me mention "lambda" (λ) and "Goodman and Kruskal's tau" (τ), which are easy to interpret because they have an upper range of 1 and a lower range of 0. "Gamma" (γ) should be consulted for ordinal data. These statistics work on a principle other than the null hypothesis, called the "proportional reduction of error," but there is no point in going into that here.[11]

There are standard computer programs to compute chi-square, lambda, tau, gamma, and many other of these statistics, along with the accompanying degrees of freedom and levels of significance where appropriate. A single DATA-TEXT control card performs this feat also. Readers with small data files, yet numerous tabulations, may wish to computerize their research if only to benefit from the machine's ability to do enormous numbers of calculations rapidly. By comparison, the calculation of chi-square by hand, as with the correlation coefficient, can be a drawn-out enterprise.

We have discussed at considerable length the two major statistics the historian may require in analyzing his output—the correlation coefficient and chi-square. The former works on quantitative interval data, the latter on qualitative nominal data. The structure of neither is difficult to understand; both may be effortlessly tabulated by computer, and by desk calculator if need be, with a modest amount of application. (See Figure 6–3 for a model depicting the relationships among various statistical methods.) As historians turn increasingly to quantitative data they will discover that a few basic graphs and charts will not exhaust the possibilities for analysis of their data. Statistics such as these provide bridges for getting from classic historical concerns about human behavior to new quantitative sources. It would be regrettable if historians permitted their visceral fear of "numerology" to stay them from attempting the crossing.

[11]For a description of these statistics see Mueller, *Statistical Reasoning in Sociology*, pp. 249–94, 432–37.

7

Conclusion:
Some Warnings

Like a Dr. Pangloss in Computerland I have guided the reader through the steps of a computer-assisted research project and sub-sequent statistical analysis of the results. Attempting to spur on the humanist, lagging after overexposure to jargon and process, I have maintained an optimistic tone. I have played down difficulties and glossed over pitfalls. Now in conclusion I should like to rectify a perhaps excessively light-hearted navigation by charting some perils.

One peril we will call orgasmic programming. It is the desire to extract from the machine, all at once, a great rush of output. The problem arises because researchers go into the output stage with an excess of enthusiasm. They revel in the prodigious capacities of the machine, which can indeed fill up entire rooms with printed results if so requested. They think, "Let's run all the variables by all the other variables to start with and see what comes out." A huge stack of paper comes forth from the high-speed printer, and that is the beginning of the analysis. Although I have demonstrated in Chapter 5 the proper steps in the first study of the results, let me indicate here what in general is wrong with orgasmic programming.

For one thing, it is usually wasteful. A certainty in this kind of re-search is that one's original research plans will turn out to be mis-guided: the scales on some of the tables will be badly proportioned;

errors in coding will turn up that render invalid all results produced to date; a special group of people, originally to have been kept separate, will turn up amongst the main population. Such deficiencies ruin the boxes of output that orgasmic programming generates, making it all garbage—expensive garbage at $300 an hour.

For another thing, orgasmic programming is intellectually offensive because it violates what is, in my mind at least, one of the cardinal precepts of quantitative analyses: One should do research by testing hypotheses, not by just cramming everything into the machine and seeing what comes out. This is not the place for an extended discourse on Shorter's View of the Scientific Method; however, I should like to indicate which of two alternative methods of analyzing results I prefer. One alternative is to proceed in an entirely *ad hoc* manner with the output. This means running one's eye over the columns of figures and acres of tables, hunting for interesting distributions or relationships. At the end of the search the scholar has a list of perhaps fifty things that have caught his eye. He muses over them and attempts to investigate them further. At the end of his labors he writes a paper in which a description of his research methods is Part A, and an account of the fascinating items he found Part B. This is, of course, a caricature of the "objective" way of doing research.

The alternative analytic procedure is to begin with a hypothesis about the event or phenomenon under study. At the very outset, ask "Did this happen because that was present?" "Were the peasants revolutionary because misery abounded in the land?" "Did Illinois go for Truman because the urban Italians hated Dewey's seigneurial mien?" Next: Call forth from the machine the basic tabulations and statistics needed to resolve that question. If the answer is yes, go on to the next question of interest; if no, formulate another hypothesis. Maybe Illinois went Democratic because the rural small-towners, not the Cicero ethnics, disliked Dewey. This approach leads us, of course, to the entire question of building models and formulating theories. I will not venture into that nether world. I am merely suggesting that posing a series of intelligent questions is the best way to get the most out of the data. How the historian chooses to present his results to his audience is his own business. My point is that orgasmic programming is incompatible with systematic problem formulation because it denies a dialogue with the computer.

The opposite of orgasmic programming is just such a dialogue. The computer permits the historian to isolate crucial kinds of evidence from his large data file, to probe and test in these sensitive areas, returning again and again to the machine with some new query arising out of past dialogues. This is the way historians normally work. They determine what diplomatic conference was decisive in launching the nations toward war, what ministerial contretemps resulted in Blatz's definitive withdrawal from the cabinet. And then they try to find out all they can about the circumstances of these critical moments, returning time and again to the source documents or to their notes. The rules of the game are not suspended when computers are involved, much as the novice researcher is tempted to command the machine: "Run everything by everything else."

A second admonition: Don't be cavalier with the data. In other words, be meticulous about cleaning up errors, running down discrepancies, double- and triple-checking, refusing to gloss over anomalies. This is more than a simple injunction to intellectual honesty. What I am saying is that the researcher should correct errors in his data even beyond the point where he is confident that such errors will not affect the reliability of his results. It is clear that in large accumulations of data a few mistakes are simply not going to make any difference. One may leave a smattering of inaccuracies in a data file and still know objectively that their distorting effect will be smoothed by the thousands and thousands (or hundreds and hundreds) of accurate cases. Nonetheless I urge: Eradicate these piddling errors as they are found even though their rectification can be of little real importance. Take the trouble to update the data tape, or to replace the erroneous cards; delay operations by a day or two while the offending mistakes are expunged, even though in the long run such compulsiveness will find no material reward. Why this counsel of anality, these exhortations to perfectionism?

In the nature of a computer study is a sense of unreality. Historians are especially prone to experience this, although scholars from other disciplines are not entirely immune either. Transcribing the world of concrete, historical experience into endless rows of numbers gives the historian the occasional feeling that he is merely juggling figures, that none of these numbers will convince anyone when the crunch finally comes, and in a publication he is supposed to associate the gossamer web of his statistical results with what happened in history. At this point the historian may undergo a minor psychological crisis: he may lose confidence in what he is doing, acutely aware of the light-years between his numbers and the flesh-and-blood people for whose actions he ultimately is trying to account. I am treating this as a psychological problem, although the opponents of quantitative history would assert it is a crippling philosophical problem as well. In this context the question becomes, how may the researcher buoy his confidence in himself and his numbers?

One practical solution is forming the resolution to be ruthless in tracking down mistakes. If the historian is able to say, "It is not possible to get any closer to the historical reality of this subject than with my data," he will be able to convince himself that he is not merely playing with numbers, that statistical differences in the means and medians of his results correspond to real differences among the groups he is studying. In short, scrupulous attention to correcting errors will help overcome the lurking feeling that one's results are artifacts of one's own making, not a reliable quantitative description of past patterns.

A third general warning is that computer research is expensive. Whereas the only extraordinary expenses historians normally encounter are getting to and from archives and photocopying sources, scholars who use computers will face a whole range of uncustomary and unexpected costs. To start with, people with substantial amounts of coding will probably want to hire research assistants in order to spare themselves some of the clerical drudgery that invariably accompanies quantitative research. Then there will be minor expenses for keypunching, although these will be among the smaller of the outlays. Next, numerous miscellaneous expenses for equipment will arise: the purchase of computer tapes, perhaps the rental of a desk calculator, binders for filing away output. Some hapless researchers will find themselves at institutions where they have to pay for computer time, the administration being too niggardly to donate it. This will run into real money, for computer time starts at $200 an hour and skyrockets from there.

The biggest cost of all is likely to be programming. I have discussed this question at some length in the section on the programming dilemma in Chapter 4, but recapitulate its basic features here.

If the historian himself is not able to write his own programs, and only a handful of historians in North America are, he will have to pay someone to do it for him. (All this, of course, applies only in the event that DATA-TEXT or some similar package of canned programs is not available.) Computer programming will occupy the largest share of the historian's project budget. Unlike keypunchers or research assistants—relatively unskilled workers and therefore plentiful and inexpensive—computer programmers command high wages. A year's salary for a full-time programmer conversant with statistics is likely to be $10,000, although the graduate students most historians will seek out would have basic pay rates considerably less than that. Hourly rates for programmers should fluctuate between $4 and $7 depending on the programmer's qualifications and on how much dead time he has to spend not using his brain but running back and forth between office and computer center or waiting for output. All this means that any project save those with absolutely minimal programming requirements will probably cost at least $1000 in programmers' salaries.

These considerations imply that in the future historians are going to be acquiring a headache long familiar to other social and natural scientists: the funding of large-scale research projects. Historians will be forced to wean themselves away from their traditional benefactors—in the United States, the American Council of Learned Societies and the Social Science Research Council, to name two of the most munificent—and to start looking elsewhere for support. They will need to accustom themselves to thinking of research requirements not in terms of subsistence and travel, but in terms of research assistance, computer time, and programming fees. This shift in research needs will necessitate a shift in the amount of funding required. Historians have traditionally thought of themselves as bold if they extended their hands for timid little sums of $500 and $1000. Such amounts will no longer be adequate for even modest quantitative projects; indeed some of the studies mentioned in the introduction will have cost over $50,000 before their findings appear in print. It appears to me there is nothing outrageous about these sums. Scholars in other disciplines have been receiving this kind of money for a long time, and now that we can justify a need for it, we should not be reticent in extending our hands.

A final caveat about finances: The historian should ask for double whatever sum he thinks at first he will need. I am not suggesting boondoggling here. Rather many people have discovered that they inevitably required more money than they anticipated. It is a general law that each step in a research project always takes longer than foreseen: designing the codebook always consumes more time than one thinks; coding always stretches out past the funds allocated; programming invariably mounts beyond original anticipations, if only because the arrival of the first output leads the historian to ask new, unanticipated questions, which in turn send the programmer back to the machine. And so forth. Nothing is more infuriating than to run out of money halfway through a project, having to stop work just as things are getting interesting because the investigator underestimated how much it would cost.

Let me divest myself of a concluding piece of advice. One hazard in working with a glittering new research implement like the computer is confusing ends and means. A real danger exists that historians may lose their perspective as they immerse themselves in this arcane technology, forgetting that machine research in particular, and quantitative techniques in general, are means to an end and not ends in themselves. Some scholars may come to think of themselves as "computer historians" and of their research as "computer projects." I feel this frame of mind is to be avoided, and nowhere in this book have I employed these terms. Perhaps I insult my readers for a final time if I remind them that as historians our first allegiance is to intellectual problems, to the unravelling of tangled sequences of causation surrounding historical events. The computer is merely one tool among many to serve this purpose. Machines must not be permitted to divert our ultimate attention from the study of men to the study of numbers.

Appendix

Several sample codebooks are reproduced here that the reader may find useful in designing his own research. The first of these I have adapted from an article by three French scholars discussing quantitative sources in the nineteenth century. Bemused by the enormous source material of the June Days arrests (12,000 dossiers) and the Paris Commune arrests of 1871 (15,000 dossiers—all stored at the archives of the Fort de Vincennes), these researchers designed a hypothetical codebook suitable for either set of data. I have made slight modifications in their effort, changing a few of the codes and adding card numbers to each card, but on the whole Sample Codebook I is merely a translation of their codebook. The second sample codebook is a version of the one Merle Curti designed for his study of the social structure of a Wisconsin county (see pp. 23–24). The third sample codebook was drawn up by Lynn Hollen Lees for her work on the Irish in Victorian London (see p. 23). Both the Curti and Lees codebooks were designed for census data.

These codebooks do not necessarily incorporate all the features I have suggested are best practice. Indeed, were their authors to design them afresh now, they would doubtless change numerous codes and fields. Nevertheless these codebooks illustrate research projects that give promise of successful conclusion.

Sample Codebook I

Arrest Dossiers for Paris June Days, 1848

CARD ONE: BIOGRAPHY

[Field]	Column	Code
1	1	Card number (1)
2	2–6	Dossier number
3	7–8	Year of arrival in France
		(Code last two digits of year)
4	9–10	Year of naturalization
		(Code last two digits of year)
5	11	Duration of military service
		(Code last two digits of year)
6	12–13	Year military service began
		(Code last two digits of year)

Adapted from A. Kriegel, R. Gossez, and J. Rougerie, "Sources et méthodes pour une histoire sociale de la classe ouvrière," *Le Mouvement social*, no. 40 (July-September, 1962), 1–18, and especially pp. 14–18. Reprinted with permission of Les Editions Ouvrières.

I have given the fields numbers by way of illustration. There is no need, however, to actually enumerate them until the programming begins, and so field designations need not be a part of the original codebook.—E.S.

CARD ONE: BIOGRAPHY (cont.)

[Field]	Column	Code
7	14–15	Department of longest military service (Code number of department) [Department codes not reproduced here]
8	16	Induction status 1 = drafted 2 = enlisted 3 = re-enlisted 4 = substitute 5 = discharged
9	17	Military rank attained 1 = homme troupe–caporal 2 = sergent–sergent chef 3 = adjudant–adjudant chef 4 = sous-lieutenant–lieutenant 5 = capitaine 6 = chef bataillon, escadron 7 = colonel–lieutenant-colonel 8 = general
10	18–19	Military assignments [Codes not reproduced here]
11	20–21	Campaigns [Codes not reproduced here]
12	22	Number of wounds (Enter actual number)
13	23	Decorations (Enter actual number)
14	24–25	First domicile in Paris [Street codes not reproduced here]
15	26–27	Duration of first domicile (in months) (Enter actual number of months)
16	28	Number of times residence changed (Enter actual number of times)
17	29–30	Most recent domicile in Paris [Street codes not reproduced here]
18	31	Duration of most recent domicile (in months) (Enter actual number of months)
19	32	Type of lodging 1 = without shelter 2 = with parents 3 = with friend 4 = with employer

[Field]	Column	Code
		5 = in dormitory room
		6 = in rooming house
		7 = sub-tenant
		8 = flat
		9 = home-owner
20	33	Floor on which lodging located
		0 = street floor
		1–5 = which upper story
21	34	Number of rooms in lodging
		(Enter actual number)
22	35	Monthly rent
		[Codes not reproduced here]
23	36	Number of months of no payment of rent
		(Enter actual number)
24	37	Height of individual
		1 = dwarf
		2 = less than 1.55 m.
		3 = 1.56–1.59 m.
		(etc.)
25	38	Distinguishing marks
		[Codes not reproduced here]
26	39–40	Physical condition
		[Codes not reproduced here]
27	41	Level of literacy
		1 = unable to sign name
		2 = able to sign name
		3 = able to read
		4 = able to write
		5 = elementary school
		6 = higher education
		7 = occupational training
28	42	Religion
		1 = agnostic
		2 = non-practicing Catholic
		3 = practicing Catholic
		4 = non-practicing Protestant
		5 = practicing Protestant
		6 = Jew
		7 = Moslem
		8 = other
29	43–44	Political opinion in 1848
		01 = Legitimist
		02 = Orleanist

sample codebook I

CARD ONE: BIOGRAPHY (cont.)

[Field]	Column	Code
		03 = Bonapartist
		04 = Republican
		05 = Democratic socialist
		06 = Communist
		07 = Fourierist
		08 = Saint Simonian
		09 = Christian socialist
		10 = Indeterminate
		11 = Not stated
30	45–46	Participation in previous political events
		[Codes not reproduced here]
31	47–48	Participiation in previous union activity
		[Codes not reproduced here]
32	49–51	Participation in strikes
		[Codes not reproduced here]
33	52–53	Interference with "freedom of labor"
		[Codes not reproduced here]
34	54–55	Department where infraction occurred
		[Department codes not reproduced here]
35	56–57	Year in which infraction occurred
		(Enter last two digits of year)
36	58	Sentence in weeks
		(Enter number of weeks)
37	59–80	Participation in June Days
		[Coding sequence not reproduced here]

CARD TWO: FAMILY STATUS

[Field]	Column	Code
	1	Card number (2)
	2–6	Dossier number
38	7	Sex
		1 = male
		2 = female
39	8–9	Year of birth
		(Enter last two digits of year)
40	10–17	Commune of birth
		(Consult official commune code list)
41	18–19	Years lived in birthplace
		(Enter actual number of years)

[Field]	Column	Code
42	20	Parentage
		1 = legitimate
		2 = illegitimate
		3 = foundling
		4 = orphaned of two parents
		5 = orphaned of father
		6 = orphaned of mother
		7 = not stated
43	21–22	Age of child at death of parents
44	23–24	Year of father's birth
		(Enter last two digits of year)
45	25–29	Canton where father born
		[Canton codes not reproduced here]
46	30–31	Department where father born
		[Department codes not reproduced here]
47	32–33	Father's occupation
		(See occupational codes)
48	34–35	Year of mother's birth
49	36–40	Canton where mother born
50	41–42	Department where mother born
51	43–44	Mother's occupation
52	45	Marital status of individual
		1 = bachelor
		2 = married
		3 = widow, widower
		4 = divorced
		5 = separated
		6 = common law
53	46–50	Canton where marriage took place
		[Canton codes not reproduced here]
54	51–52	Year of marriage
		(Enter last two digits of year)
55	53–54	Year of divorce
		(Enter last two digits of year)
56	55–56	Year of spouse's birth
		(Enter last two digits of year)
57	57–61	Canton where spouse born
58	62–66	Canton where spouse domiciled
59	67–68	Occupation of spouse
60	69	Total number of children
		(Enter actual number)

CARD TWO: FAMILY STATUS (cont.)

[Field]	Column	Code
61	70–71	Year of birth of first child
		(Enter last two digits of year)
62	72–73	Year of birth of second child
63	74–75	Year of birth of third child
64	76–77	Year of birth of fourth child
65	78–79	Year of birth of fifth child
	80	BLANK

CARD THREE: OCCUPATION

[Field]	Column	Code
	1	Card number (3)
	2–6	Dossier number
66	7–8	First occupation
		[Occupational codes not reproduced here]
67	9–10	Year in which occupation changed (most important change, if several made—enter last two digits of year)
68	11	Number of occupations practiced
69	12–13	Most recent occupation practiced
70	14	First social status
		[Social status codes not reproduced here]
71	15–16	Year in which status changed (most important change, if several made—enter last two digits of year)
72	17	Number of changes of status
73	18	Most recent status
74	19–20	Duration of apprenticeship (in months) (Code actual number of months)

FIRST EMPLOYMENT

[Field]	Column	Code
75	21–25	Canton where apprenticeship or first job served [Canton codes not reproduced here]
76	26	Mode of remuneration
		1 = piece work
		2 = hourly
		3 = daily
		4 = salaried
77	27	Mean daily salary (Enter actual figure)

CARD THREE: OCCUPATION (cont.)

[Field]	Column	Code
78	28–29	Duration of first job (in months) (Enter actual number of months)
79	30–31	Duration of unemployment (Enter actual number of weeks)

SECOND EMPLOYMENT

[Field]	Column	Code
80–84	32–42	(See codes and fields for first employment; not reproduced here for lack of space)

THIRD EMPLOYMENT

[Field]	Column	Code
85–89	43–53	(See codes and fields for first employment)

FOURTH EMPLOYMENT

[Field]	Column	Code
90–94	54–64	(See codes and fields for first employment)

FIFTH EMPLOYMENT

[Field]	Column	Code
95–99	65–75	(See codes and fields for first employment)
100	76	Number of jobs held in Paris
101	77–78	Year of arrival in Paris (Code last two digits of year)
102	79–80	Week of arrival in Paris (Code number of week)

CARD FOUR: TRIAL

[Field]	Column	Code
	1	Card number (4)
103	2	First jurisdiction court
		1 = cour appel sur appel de Tribunal Correctionnel
		2 = cour appel sur appel de Tribunal de Simple Police
		3 = cour d'Assises
		4 = tribunal de police correctionnelle
		5 = tribunal de simple police
		6 = jurisdiction pour enfants
		7 = Conseil de guerre (ou Tribunal Militaire)
		8 = Commission militaire (ou Commission mixte)
		9 = Cours des Paris (ou Haute Cour)
104	3–4	Court of appeal [Codes not reproduced here]

sample codebook I

CARD FOUR: TRIAL (cont.)

[Field]	Column	Code
105	5–6	Department where first jurisdiction court sat [Codes not reproduced here]
106	7–9	Municipality where first jurisdiction court sat (See official geographic codes)
107	10–14	Dossier number
108	15–16	Week of decision (Enter number of week)
109	17–18	Year of decision (Enter last two digits of year)
110	19	Mode of judgment 1 = contradictoire 2 = contumace
111	20–21	Sentence [Sentence codes not reproduced here]
112	22	Reprieve 1 = with reprieve 2 = without reprieve 3 = not stated
113	23	Sojourn forbidden 1 = yes 2 = no 3 = banishment
114	24–26	Principal crime [Crime codes not reproduced here]
115	27–28	Date of liberation (Calculated in number of months elapsed since sentencing)

The remaining columns on this card duplicate the above information for succeeding trials.

Sample Codebook II

Coding of Census for 1860 and 1870 in Trempealeau County, Wisconsin

Column	Code
1	Census year
	5 = 1850 census
	6 = 1860 census
	7 = 1870 census
	8 = 1880 census
2–3	Township or village of residence
	01 = Arcadia
	02 = Burnside
	03 = Caledonia
	(etc., up to township 23)
4–7	Individual serial number
8–9	Age of subject in years
	(Where the person is not a householder, these columns are overstruck with XX)

Adapted from Merle Curti, *The Making of an American Community* (Stanford, Calif.: Stanford University Press, 1959), pp. 451–55. Reprinted by permission of the Stanford University Press.

Column	Code
10–11	Occupation of subject
	(Where the subject is a woman, these columns are over-struck with XX)
	[The code provides for 99 separate occupations; it is not reproduced here]
12–14	Value of real property of subject in hundreds of dollars
15–18	Value of personal property of subject in tens of dollars
19–20	Birthplace of subject
	[Detailed code not reproduced here. Numbers 1–44 stand for American states; 45–47 assigned to Commonwealth; 58–66 to Central European States, and so on.]
21–22	Birthplace of subject's spouse
23–24	Number of dependents
25	Number of servants in household
26	Number of apprentices or agricultural laborers in household
27	Literacy
	1 = cannot read
	2 = cannot write
	3 = can neither read nor write
	6 = cannot read or write (ambiguous record, 1860 only)
28	Number of boys age 5–17 in household
29	Number of boys age 5–17 who attended school within the year
30	Number of girls age 5–17 in household
31	Number of girls age 5–17 who attended school within the year
32	None, some, or all children age 5–17 attending school within the year
	1 = no children of school age attended school during year
	2 = some children 5–17 attended
	3 = all children 5–17 attended
33	Nativity group
34	Occupational group
35	Birthplace of parents
	1 = both parents foreign-born
	2 = both parents American-born
	3 = father foreign-born, mother native
	4 = mother foreign-born, father native
36–38	Number improved acres
39–41	Number acres woodland
42–44	Number unimproved acres
45–47	Cash values of subject's farm in hundreds of dollars
48–50	Value of farm implements in tens of dollars
51–52	Expenditures of farm wages during year in tens of dollars
53–54	Number of cows
55–56	Number of sheep

sample codebook II

Column	Code
57–58	Number of swine
59–61	Value of livestock in tens of dollars
62–63	Number bushels of wheat in hundreds of dollars
64–67	Total value of farm produce in tens of dollars
68–69	Alphabetical group

["This code was devised to facilitate the identification of persons who were present in two or more consecutive census periods." The complete code is not reproduced here.]

Column	Code
70–72	Total property, real and personal, in hundreds of dollars
73–75	Total number acres reported
76–79	Value of farm per acre
80	Persistence

0 = present 1860, 1870, and 1880
1 = present 1860 and 1870
2 = present 1870 and 1880

Sample Codebook III

The Irish in Victorian London, Censuses of 1851 and 1861

Column	Item
1	Source Number
	1 = HO-107 (1851)
	2 = RG-9 (1861)
2–3	Location: registration district
	[1–37 See extra sheet—not reproduced here]
4	Location: subdistrict and parish
	[1–9 See extra sheet—not reproduced here]
5–6	Street
	[1–99 See extra sheet—not reproduced here]
7–9	Page number in census book
10–12	Official Household Number
	(Enter enumerator's number)
13–16	Consecutive Household Number

This codebook is reproduced courtesy of Lynn Hollen Lees; preliminary findings of this study were reported in "Patterns of Lower-Class Life: Irish Slum Communities in Nineteenth-Century London," in Stephan Thernstrom and Richard Sennett, eds., *Nineteenth-Century Cities: Essays in the New Urban History* (New Haven: Yale University Press, 1969), pp. 359–85.

Column	Item

17–18   Card Number

         (Each member of household is given a consecutive number)

19–20   Status of Individual within household

         (See extra sheet A)

21   Sex and marital status

         1 = married male

         2 = unmarried male

         3 = married female

         4 = unmarried female

         5 = widower

         6 = widow

         7 = unknown

22–23   Age

         (Enter actual number)

24–25   Occupation: industrial group

         (See extra sheet B)

26–27   Occupation: social class

         (See extra sheets B and D)

28–29   Birthplace

         [See extra sheet—not reproduced here]

30–43   Name

         (Enter family name, then given name)

44–46   House number

         (Enter actual number)

47   Family type

         (See extra sheet C)

48–49   Number in head's family

         (Count nuclear family only)

50–51   Number in head's household

52   Number of households in house

         (1–9   Enter actual number)

         [10 and above.   See extra sheet—not reproduced here]

53–54   Number of persons in house

         [See extra sheet for numbers over 99—not reproduced here]

55–56   Number of Irish-born in house

         [See extra sheet for numbers over 99—not reproduced here]

57–58   Number of children in head's family

59   Number of other relatives in head's family

60–61   Number of lodgers in household

62   Number of servants in household

63–64   Number of visitors in household

65–72   Former residences of head and family

         (Code up to four 2-digit numbers. See Birthplace sheet for codes)

Column	Item

73–76   Range of years for arrival in England
          (Code mean and estimate of error in years)
77–80   Range of years for arrival in London
          (Code mean and estimate of error in years)

EXTRA SHEET A:
STATUS WITHIN THE HOUSEHOLD (Columns 19–20)

01 = Head
02 = Wife
03 = Son
04 = Daughter
05 = Sister
06 = Brother
07 = Mother
08 = Father
09 = Grandchild
10 = Nephew
11 = Niece
12 = Aunt
13 = Uncle
14 = Brother-in-law
15 = Sister-in-law
16 = Father-in-law
17 = Mother-in-law
18 = Other relatives
51 = Grandmother
52 = Son or daughter-in-law
21 = Servant
53 = Servant's child
22 = Visitor
30 = Visitor's wife
31 = Visitor's child
32 = Visitor's brother
48 = Visitor's sister
33 = Visitor's parent
34 = Visitor's other relative
23 = Apprentice
24 = Shop assistant, employee
55 = Pupil
49 = Other
54 = Other's family
67 = Head of police station
68 = Prisoner
50 = Unknown

20 = Lodger in Irish family
25 = Lodger's wife in Irish family
26 = Lodger's child in Irish family
27 = Lodger's brother in Irish family
28 = Lodger's sister in Irish family
29 = Lodger's parent in Irish family
44 = Lodger's other relative in
     Irish family
35 = Lodger in non-Irish family
36 = Lodger's wife in non-Irish
     family
37 = Lodger's child in non-Irish
     family
38 = Lodger's other relative in
     non-Irish family
56 = Lodger in lodging house
57 = Lodger's wife in lodging house
58 = Lodger's child in lodging
     house
59 = Lodger's other relative in
     lodging house
40 = Visitor in non-Irish family
41 = Visitor's wife in non-Irish
     family
42 = Visitor's child in non-Irish
     family
43 = Visitor's other relative in
     non-Irish family
45 = Servant in non-Irish family
46 = Apprentice in non-Irish family
47 = Shop assistant or employee in
     non-Irish family

EXTRA SHEET B:
OCCUPATIONS (Columns 24–25)

Industrial Groups	Social Groups
01 = Agriculture	01 = Professional
02 = Mining	02 = Sub-professional
03 = Construction	03 = Owner, entrepreneur
04 = Metalwork	04 = Sub-managerial
05 = Machinery, tools, instruments, vehicles	05 = Employee, clerk
	06 = Agriculture—self-employed
06 = Ships	07 = Agriculture—tenant
07 = Gas, chemicals, fuel	08 = Agriculture—laborer
08 = Glass, minerals, pottery	09 = High commercant
09 = Textiles	10 = Shopkeeper, petty entrepreneur
10 = Dress	
11 = Leather, animal products	11 = Hawker, pedlar
12 = Wood, furniture	12 = Skilled labor
13 = Paper, vegetable products	13 = Semiskilled labor
14 = Printing, engraving	14 = Unskilled labor
15 = Food	15 = Jobless
16 = Transport—communications	16 = Rentier, independent means
17 = Transport—docks and canals	17 = Annuitant
18 = Transport—railways and roads	18 = Supported by family
19 = Transport—goods	19 = Student
20 = General labor	20 = Social outcast
21 = Commerce	21 = Small child
22 = Service occupations	22 = Retired
23 = Domestic service	23 = No occupation
24 = Administration	33 = Unknown
25 = Military	31 = Other
26 = Police and prisons	
27 = Professions	
28 = Art, literature, science, education	
29 = Entertainment	
30 = Outside the labor market	
31 = Other	
33 = Unknown	
34 = Finance and banking	

EXTRA SHEET C:
FAMILY TYPE (Column 47)

1 = Nuclear family only
2 = Nuclear family assisted

sample codebook III

EXTRA SHEET C: (cont'd)

3 = Nuclear family dependency
4 = Nuclear family assisted and dependency
5 = Extended nuclear only
6 = Extended nuclear assisted
7 = Extended nuclear dependency
8 = Extended nuclear assisted and dependency
9 = Single member only
A = Single member multiple
B = Single member assisted
C = Single member dependency
D = Single member assisted and dependency
E = Single member multiple, assisted and dependency
F = Single member multiple and assisted

EXTRA SHEET D:
BREAKDOWN OF CATEGORIES FOR OCCUPATION:
SOCIAL CLASS (Columns 26–27)

01 = PROFESSIONAL—lawyer, doctor, Church of England minister, independent educator, architect, army officer, magistrate, dentist
02 = SUBPROFESSIONAL—teacher, nurse, nonconformist minister, artist,
musician, archbishop's secretary, surveyor, curate, veterinary doctor,
low rank military officer, druggist, newspaper editor
03 = OWNER-ENTREPRENEUR—large landowner, shipowner, manager or
owner of a business employing more than four people, owner of more
than one business
04 = SUBMANAGERIAL—office supervisor, police sergeant, head clerk,
auditor, accountant, tax collector, reporter, railroad inspector, auc-
tioneer, parish clerk, Poor Law administrator, land agent, factor, master mariner, ballast master, middle-grade post office official
05 = EMPLOYEE AND CLERICAL—white-collar employee, clerk, customs
office, tide waiter, fireman, police constable, shop assistant
06 = AGRICULTURE: SELF-EMPLOYED—independent farmer, yeoman,
small land owner
07 = AGRICULTURE: TENANT—tenant, overseer
08 = AGRICULTURE: LABORER—farm worker, hop picker, day laborer
09 = HIGH COMMERCANT—merchant, broker, financier of any sort
10 = SHOPKEEPER—petty entrepreneur (those employing under five people),
publican, lodging house keeper, shopkeeper
11 = HAWKER—pedlar, scavenger, street dealer
12 = SKILLED LABOR—all craftsmen, artisans, soldier, sailor, dressmaker,
seamstress, translator
13 = SEMISKILLED LABOR—domestic servant, journeyman, apprentice,

carman, waiter, steward, animal tender, laundress, gardener, brickman, scissors grinder, slop worker, coal whipper, cord and rope maker, pickler, shoe black, stevedore, steamboat stoker, ballast heaver, feather dresser (See Armstrong for others)

14 = UNSKILLED—general laborer, dock laborer, dustman, porter, errand boy, news vendor, charwoman, watchman, rag picker, crossing sweeper, wood chopper, messenger

15 = UNEMPLOYED—only those listed as jobless, unemployed

16 = RENTIER, INDEPENDENT MEANS—lady, gentleman, "of independent income," stockholder

17 = ANNUITANT—pensioner, annuitant

18 = SUPPORTED BY FAMILY—any child over five, relative, female, old person with no occupation listed in a household with employed members

19 = STUDENT—anyone in school

20 = SOCIAL OUTCAST—pauper, beggar, prostitute, thief

21 = SMALL CHILD—child of five years or under

22 = RETIRED—retired

23 = NO OCCUPATION

31 = OTHER

33 = UNKNOWN

Index

Scattergram, 107, 110, 111
Shapiro, Gilbert, 20
Shover, John L., 15
Significance (statistical), 109, 117–18
Skewness, 96–97
Social structure, 4, 22–24
"Sociological" history, 19–27
Sorter (*see* IBM punchcard, counter-sorter)
Stone, Lawrence, 46

Tau (statistic), 119
Telescoping codes, 39–45
Textual analysis, 20, 76n
Thernstrom, Stephan, 2n, 24
Tilly, Charles, 2n, 20–22, 43–45, 82n

"Twelve-edge," 29

Unit of analysis, 33, 35, 78
Urban history, 3, 22–24

Value (statistical), 83–84
Variable, 36
Variance, analysis of, 113

Warner, Sam Bass, Jr., 24
Wrigley, E. A., 26

Zone punching area, 29, 34